*daily gems
to spark
your spirit*

daily gems to spark your spirit

a little bright light for your day!

Donna M. Liples

daily gems to spark your spirit

Trilogy Christian Publishers A Wholly Owned Subsidiary of Trinity Broadcasting Network

2442 Michelle Drive Tustin, CA 92780

Copyright © 2021 by Donna M. Liples

Scripture quotations marked AMP are taken from the Amplified® Bible (AMP), Copyright © 2015 by The Lockman Foundation. Used by permission. www.Lockman.org.

Scripture quotations marked KJV are taken from the King James Version of the Bible. Public domain.

Scripture quotations marked NIV are taken from the Holy Bible, New International Version®, NIV®. Copyright © 1973, 1978, 1984, 2011 by Biblica, Inc.TM Used by permission of Zondervan. All rights reserved worldwide. www.zondervan.com. The "NIV" and "New International Version" are trademarks registered in the United States Patent and Trademark Office by Biblica, Inc.TM

Scripture quotations marked NKJV are taken from the New King James Version®. Copyright © 1982 by Thomas Nelson. Used by permission. All rights reserved.

Scripture quotations marked NLT are taken from the Holy Bible, New Living Translation, copyright © 1996, 2004, 2015 by Tyndale House Foundation. Used by permission of Tyndale House Publishers, Inc., Carol Stream, Illinois 60188. All rights reserved.

No part of this book may be reproduced, stored in a retrieval system, or transmitted by any means without written permission from the author. All rights reserved. Printed in the USA.

Rights Department, 2442 Michelle Drive, Tustin, CA 92780.

Trilogy Christian Publishing/TBN and colophon are trademarks of Trinity Broadcasting Network.

For information about special discounts for bulk purchases, please contact Trilogy Christian Publishing.

Trilogy Disclaimer: The views and content expressed in this book are those of the author and may not necessarily reflect the views and doctrine of Trilogy Christian Publishing or the Trinity Broadcasting Network.

Manufactured in the United States of America

10 9 8 7 6 5 4 3 2 1

Library of Congress Cataloging-in-Publication Data is available.

ISBN: 978-1-64773-857-0

E-ISBN: 978-1-64773-858-7

To God be the glory.

To my husband, Ron, forty years is a long time to be hopeful that this would happen! Thank you!

To our sons, Aaron and Eliot, daughters-in-love, Robin and Marie, and to our four grandchildren, Jaron, Evan, Grant, and Preston, thank you for your fun stories, photos, insights, and inspiration right when I needed some.

To Katie, the friend I haven't met yet. I am not sure you know how much you have motivated me to begin writing again. When I had pretty much given up the idea, you became my incarcerated pen-pal. That was the motivation I needed to begin writing again. Thank you.

contents

amethyst—thankful 13
    body beautiful 15
    fire on the beach 17
    i am undone 19
    mother's day is coming 21
    only 10%? what about the rest? 25
    sardi's hope 29
    sing! 33
    the race of life 35
    who am i in Christ? 39
    worry? not me! 41

aquamarine—forgiveness 43
    be joyful, patient, prayerful, repeat! 45
    bless you 47
    bread of life 49
    guilty as charged! 53
    improve your smile 57
    judge and jury 59
    let's run 63
    live at peace with everyone 65
    queen esther in lancaster county 67
    healing through the ten commandments 71

diamond—home 73
    a party invitation 75
    are we there yet? 77
    are you contaminated? 79
    do you believe this? 81
    guardians of the force 83

he is risen! just as he said.	87
hello march!	91
is this the end?	93
plus ultra	97
sparkling!	99

emerald—trusting   103

bloom where God has re-planted you	105
my Christmas wishlist	107
f.a.i.t.h.	109
how are your casting skills?	113
it's in there	115
that's impossible	117
transformers: more than meets the eye!	119
what are you leaning on?	123
what do we do now?	125
wings	127

garnet—steadfast   129

do. or do not. there is no try.	131
do you want to be a model?	135
prayer: focus	137
it's the truth, ruth	141
king of the mountain	145
my rock obsession	147
sacrifice	149
seek his face	151
somebody's always watching you!	153
the triplets	155

opal—kindness 159
   april hope 161
   be an overcomer! 163
   divine appointment? 165
   do you have a gift for me? 169
   ezer 173
   gimmie that! i want it! 177
   God is more than enough! 179
   handprints everywhere! 181
   compound blessings 183
   mission: focus 185
   we light up the world 189

pearl—heroes 191
   eighty-five and alive! 193
   dad and donna marie 197
   give me liberty or give me… 199
   happy birthday, anna! 201
   happy birthday, united states! 205
   hosanna! praise him! 209
   laus deo 213
   memories… 215
   penn's woods 217
   presidential ponderings 219

ruby—love 221
   all in a day's work 223
   amadao 225
   butterfly kisses 227
   chosen! 229
   he's right there! 231

hi nana!	235
humble love; maundy thursday	237
i hate...	241
up, up, and away!	243
yummy marinate recipe	245
sapphire—faithful	**249**
1975	251
don't pray about it	255
exposed	257
frigid to fire	259
gps: God's protection system	261
just ask me!	263
listen!	265
looking in the rearview mirror	267
lots o' dots	269
promises	271
afterword	**273**

preface

I am glad that you chose my book of devotionals! I trust that the next ninety days' readings will be encouraging to you, and a "firelight" on your path. I have heard from several people that they find it difficult jumping right in to reading the Bible. Where do I begin? How can I find something relevant for me? How does this book relate to my life? Here in *daily gems to spark your spirit*, I have divided the devotionals into categories. I expect this will make it easier when you want a scripture reading that addresses a certain issue. You can begin there, then the story will bring the verse to a place you can use in your life. You can begin anywhere you would like to, as the pages are not dated. Or you can start at the beginning and go through the three months of devotionals. Either way, I am sure you will find the Word speaking to your heart.

In my many years teaching on Bible topics, I found that just the reading of the scripture, though very valuable all by itself, is not always enough to get that scripture to "stick" in your heart. By adding an anecdote, a problem, or funny story with the scripture, there is a greater opportunity to remember it and apply it to your life when you need it. It can be pulled back out of that file where it is stored in your head and applied where needed. The situations in my book are ones so many of us have experienced I expect you will see that "connection" being made right then.

At the beginning of 2020, I began a daily blog of devotionals. As I continued to write, I received comments about writing a book of devotionals. After a couple more months, and the Lord prompting me, I decided to jump in.

This is my first book of devotionals. I would like to hear your feedback. I will be praying for you, though I don't know who you are, the Lord knows. I trust Him to pour out the blessing of His presence as you read!

amethyst—thankful

body beautiful

For as in one body we have many members, but all the members have not the same office; so we, the many, are one body in Christ, and every one members one of another. The illustration of the body with its members to set forth the mutual dependence on each other of the several members of the Church with their several gifts and functions, and the importance of all for the well-being.

Romans 12:4-5 (KJV)

Today, I want to give you a chuckle. An expression my husband uses when we talk about two families living in one house: "It's like putting two feet in one shoe." Now, if you get a vision of that like I do, not only is it uncomfortable, but it is quite inefficient. For example, two cooks living in one household decide to each make their favorite dish for the family. When each begins the cooking process, the kitchen becomes alive with aprons, bowls, ingredients, and recipes. I know when my husband and I try this, it's a disaster! He gets out three eggs to use in his recipe. I only need one and take one of the eggs on the counter. I get out our large mixing bowl to make my recipe, he needs it for his and leaves me without. I need to use every burner for the different parts of my masterpiece. He needs one, but there are none for him. You can imagine the tension in that kitchen!

This would quickly become a comedy of errors if we thought it was funny! Now, if we talk to each other before we start, we can split up the tasks. Today you cook, I'll set the table and clean up. Tomorrow, we will reverse that process. This is what we do now after trying it the other way!

Imagine in a larger organization if everyone is talented in the hiring position. All day these job recruiters' interview and hire people to do, well, the job they are already doing themselves. When Monday rolls around and the work needs to be done, no one is prepared to do it. Oh, they are doing their job; they are hiring more people to hire people! Or, in a hospital setting everyone is a surgeon. Well, we can see how that won't work. The surgeon suits up for surgery, but where is the patient? Since everyone is trained to be the doctor, no one brought the patient to the operating room on a gurney, prepped the patient, anesthetized the patient, or even checked the patient's vitals. The doctors just want to perform the surgery!

It's no different in a church. If all the people want to be on the worship team to sing and play an instrument, who would preach? Who would they preach to? If all we want to do was sit in the congregation and listen, who would we listen to? We can clearly see that a division of jobs and responsibilities is necessary; in fact, it's essential. And each one of the divisions of labor is essential.

I wish I knew this a long time ago. As a teen I had a talent for sewing, crafting, and writing. I didn't view these as "gifts from God." As a result, I did not try to perfect these talents and just saw them as hobbies.

When the Lord gives us our gift, calling, or talent, it's ours to keep. He will not take it back, but what we do with it is our responsibility. Investing time and treasure into honing it into something God can use for His glory is worth the effort. Let us ask God what gifts He has given us, then do our best to work at making them the best we can for Him. Each part of the body, when used in its own unique gift, is beautiful and makes the world a much better place.

Question: What are your gifts? How are you using them?

fire on the beach

For in this hope we were saved. But hope that is seen is no hope at all. Who hopes for what they already have? But if we hope for what we do not yet have, we wait for it patiently.

Romans 8:24 (NIV)

One evening when we were at the shore, we watched as the earth got tired and closed her eyes to the day. The sunset constantly changed colors. I knew I was watching a master artist as He splashed orange, terracotta, and burnt sienna against the azure sky. The yellow ball we call the sun in the day turned into a fiery indescribable shape as it slowly dropped down out of sight. A small sliver of red remained reminding us the sun was gone but not for long!

People were still gathered on the beach, but then they drew closer. Soon, I could see fire pits beginning to pop up as the people gathered in semi-circles. I felt like I was watching the end of the day at a campground. I could almost hear, "Kumbaya, My Lord" as they asked the Lord to "come near me" and the day turned into night.

Other fires popped up on the shore, and soon after I couldn't see people any longer, I saw flames! It was a truly inspiring sight as the fire pit flames lit the shore, and the unseen waves continued to roar and then slap down on the sand. Each slap drawing a layer of sand out into the water until the next wave returned it to the shore. As I watched, a deep appreciation began to well up in my soul. Listening but not seeing those waves continue over and over again somehow gave me hope!

See, that continuing roar, slap, woosh of those waves I could not see reminded me that everything God has promised to us after we die is unseen. Yet, we believe. Why? Because we see the proof of His integrity in this continuing earth. We hear the next generation in a baby's cry. We see a beautiful future in a graduate. We share the joy of a man and woman at the altar so innocent, yet hopeful for a bright beginning together. Years later we watch them as they cling to each other after their child died. We watch as an elderly couple still smiles at each other giving a morning kiss. At the grave site he reluctantly tosses a rose on her grave, her favorite flower. He promises he will be with her soon.

In all of our lives, the constant of nature reminds us we are not alone. Whatever happens to us, the sun will set one day and rise the next. The ocean will roar, whether we see it or not. And there will still be campfires on the beach with a gentle request: "come near me, Lord, come near me."

Question: What memory do you have that instills that feeling of hope for a better tomorrow?

i am undone!

Praise the LORD. Praise God in his sanctuary; praise him in his mighty heavens. Praise him for his acts of power; praise him for his surpassing greatness. Praise him with the sounding of the trumpet, praise him with the harp and lyre, praise him with timbrel and dancing, praise him with the strings and pipe, praise him with the clash of cymbals, praise him with resounding cymbals. Let everything that has breath Praise the Lord. Praise the LORD!

Psalm 150 1-6 (NIV)

After our five-and-a-half-hour trip to Ocean City, Maryland, my husband and I were beat! It was 87 degrees when we left Pennsylvania, the SUV was packed, the plans were made, and we had great expectations of a few day wonderful getaway. Between the road, the heat, the traffic, and even the other drivers, the drive took its toll on us! We were tired, sore, and cranky.

We arrived at this unfamiliar place, and now the luggage had to go up five floors. Hubby managed get the luggage in the elevator with a wobbly rebellious cart. I started sanitizing, nesting, unpacking, and putting our things in convenient places. I tried to make this a comfortable home away from home.

We heated up our dinner, ate, and cleaned up after. We then went to the main event: the ocean! Our first glimpse of the ocean brought tears to my eyes. The roar of each wave as it pounded on the sand just overfilled my senses. The blue-gray streaks of the water lapping at the tlatte-colored beach.

We walked along the shoreline, but after a few feet, I stopped. My husband asked, "What's wrong? Why are you stopping?" I looked out at that magnificent body of water and remembered Psalm 150 (NIV). Praise the Lord! "I am undone," I my replied, "This makes it all worth it."

That was all I wanted to do: praise! I wanted to yell out my praise to my God. The God who not only created the sea and everything in it but also created me to be able to enjoy it.

I might have been imagining it, but I looked up and thought I saw God smile at me as I praised Him and thanked Him for His indescribable creation!

It is not often that we are just swept away by the wonder of God's creation, but the first glimpse at the ocean always does it for me.

O Lord, my words cannot even come close to describing your magnificent creation. You know how my heart is filled to overflowing with awe and admiration for your creativity. Please accept my praise as an act of worship to You!

Question: Is there a specific scene that brings you to that place I call "undone" where there are no words to describe your awe of God?

mother's day is coming!

> Dear children, let us not love with words or speech, but with actions and truth.
>
> 1 John 3:18 (NIV)

I don't know what emotion the title brings in your heart. Is it fear: "Oh no, it's Mother's Day already" Is it joy, "Mother's Day! Let's plan a special day for Mom." Or is it a sad reminder that your mom is no longer here? Whatever emotion surfaces, please remember your mother.

When I was a kid, I paid very close attention to these holidays. For days, I would save my "milk money" at school, then take my money to the Woolworth store that was a block away. For those of you too young to know about Woolworth, it was a type of Walmart. I would peruse the aisles looking for just the right gift for my mom. Maybe it was a new color of nail polish; maybe it was a new knick-knack or a necklace or scarf.

No matter how cheap and useless the gift was, Mom always said, "Oh, it's just what I wanted." Because she understood the amount of effort that I had invested in it with my love.

When I became a mom, I would make suggestions to my two boys. Boys did not always have the insight of a girl, and I did not want to be disappointed. I would throw out hints beginning a few days before Mother's Day, loudly proclaiming within earshot of my husband and sons, "Wow, this garage could really use a good cleaning by some strong boys," or, "I am amazed at how the weeds have just sprung up in the side flower beds. I guess I will have to go out and weed them soon." You get the picture. I was ecstatic when they got the hints, and they were ecstatic that "they" thought of something I wanted! Win-win!

Now, I am a grandma. Parents raising children are very busy with their own careers and activities with their children and spouses. I have every "creature comfort" I need. What I want is their time. Time to find out what is going on in their lives. Time to chat about the good old days but only for a little bit. I want to hear the new world things that my grandchildren are learning. What is the latest fashion from my granddaughter? What are her hopes, dreams, plans for the future? The boys still like to talk about the Legos they built, the last *Star Wars* movie they saw (five times) or a new planet or dinosaur that has been discovered.

Today's verse says don't be a talker of good deeds, show some action! Three generations of children serving Mom on her day. I do like any day that I can spend with my children and grandchildren knowing that it is a fun time to spend time with mom/nana. I don't ever want it to be a chore or a requirement. When these days end, I will go back and revisit them in my memory and smile!

When our Heavenly Father says, in His Word, that He wants to spend time with us, I believe His desire is to catch-up with us too! Our time together is a joy, a privileged, a special time to look forward to. He wants to catch up with us. What are we learning in His word? What new hobby do we have or friend did we meet? He is also a hint giver, telling us, "See that family? They are struggling and need a helping hand with some groceries." Or telling us the young woman two doors down has questions about her faith walk and you can answer her questions.

Bottom line, God made us to be "relational" because we are made in His image, and He is relational. So, go ahead, pour your heart out to your Heavenly Father. He will savor the time together and remember it later and enjoy it again! By the way, so will your mom!

mother's day is coming!

Question: So, what were your favorite times with your Mom? Can you share them with her? She would probably like to know. I know I would. Hint-hint.

only 10%? what about the rest?

Rejoice always, pray continually, give thanks in all circumstances; for this is God's will for you in Christ Jesus.

1 Thessalonians 5:16-18 (NIV)

Ever see those vintage neon "Thank You" signs outside a little shop? Sometimes I think we need to have one of those signs in our view all the time. I know it can be difficult to understand why we say "thank you" to God when it feels like we were really handed a very bad blow. Yet, that is what our verse for today tells us, "give thanks in all circumstances."

In the spring, I am always reminded of my niece and nephew. A beautiful and joyful Christian couple were finally able to give birth to the son of their dreams, Dominic, on May 1. After eight years of investing love and everything parents want to bestow on their children, he was diagnosed with a rare brain cancer. Everyone began to pray, intercede, and help any way we could, but in the end, nine months later, he returned to the arms of Jesus.

Are we expected to say "thank you" then? Yes, even then. How? Parents, grandparents, aunts, uncles, cousins were broken-hearted, right to our core. Though it was so difficult right then, it eventually happened. At the memorial service, held in the school auditorium, people spoke about how this one little boy improved their lives. They talked about how Dominic was cheerful, funny, and grateful even in pain. That's when we could say "thank you."

You, Lord, gave us Dominic through miraculous circumstances (as in every birth). You, Lord, knew what family he could live with for his short eight years and be loved and nurtured. Thank You! You,

Lord, put people in his path through his illness that he would share his faith in Jesus in his innocent way. Because of Dominic, some of them did too.

When Jesus was on earth for His brief time, He healed so many people. In one group alone, He healed ten.

> Now on his way to Jerusalem, Jesus traveled along the border between Samaria and Galilee. As he was going into a village, ten men who had leprosy met him. They stood at a distance and called out in a loud voice, "Jesus, Master, have pity on us!" When he saw them, he said, "Go, show yourselves to the priests." And as they went, they were cleansed. One of them, when he saw he was healed, came back, praising God in a loud voice. He threw himself at Jesus' feet and thanked him-and he was a Samaritan. Jesus asked, "Were not all ten cleansed? Where are the other nine? Has no one returned to give praise to God except this foreigner?" Then he said to him, "Rise and go; your faith has made you well."
>
> Luke 17:11-19 (NIV)

Ten percent! Seems rather a small number of people when you consider the magnitude of what Jesus did for them. Thank you, a grateful heart, and appreciation for something we cannot do of our own will. We need God's intervention.

I found another pithy statement that really hit me, no, it clobbered me! "What if you woke up today with only the things you thanked God for yesterday?"

My niece and nephew thanked God every step of their journey with Dominic, and every day they were able to spend with him. Our Lord just wants gratitude for what He gives us. Like a parent who gives so much, a simple "thanks Mom" goes a long way!

"Though he slay me, yet will I hope in him; I will surely defend my ways to his face" (Job 13:15, NIV)

We are in a crazy time in our nation right now. How do we thank God for this? Well, we know God didn't bring this on us. He only gives good gifts. Therefore, He is the one protecting, helping, providing, comforting, serving, and giving us hope in Him!

Thank You, Lord, and thank You again! Through this crazy time, you continue to be with us, provide and comfort us. You remind us of what You have done in our past, and we read of all the times You intervened in people's lives in the Bible, in history, and in our own families. Thank You Lord, and please, do it again!

Question: Have *you* thanked God today?

sardi's hope

The King will reply, "Truly I tell you, whatever you did for one of the least of these brothers and sisters of mine, you did for me."

Matthew 25:40 (NIV)

I haven't ever really had an interest in the Caribbean. Oh, I know people who have come from there, and I really like them. I do enjoy looking at the beaches and looking at items that come from there, even trying their foods. I just wasn't ever interested in going there. Until...

One day a dear friend of mine was collecting things from people at church in big bags. Being my usual curious, or nosy, self, I asked her what she was collecting. Now, the collecting part isn't unusual. We collect plastic grocery bags to be made into mats for homeless, empty water bottles to redeem for a nickel each, bottle lids to recycle into playground equipment, hygiene products for prisoners, and on and on. You get the idea. But this was a bag full of clothes for something I had not been introduced to before: the Dominican Republic. I wanted in.

My good friend told me of families in the Dominican Republic that live below the poverty level in virtual shacks while government employees live at a much higher standard. There is no help from the government there like is here in the states with food stamps and other helps for those in need. This child in the photo, Sardi, is literally chewing on a dog bone!

When I see this type of image, and hear the story, I am moved with compassion. "What can I do to help alleviate someone's suffering," I asked my friend. The Lord has blessed be beyond measure, I want to give back.

Here are some ways we can help:

Pray: God has not forgotten them, but they may be so engrossed in just surviving, that prayer may not be on their radar, so we must pray!

Donate: If you have summer clothes that are still in good condition and you want to give them away, please find a place near you that takes care of the homeless.

Sew: If you can sew, there are simple dress you can make from pillowcases. My mom is making pillowcase dresses we are sending to the Dominican Republic. Africa also has great need for them. Check out the internet for ideas in "sewing for charity." You can call a local women's shelter to help with food, clothes, toys, and many other needs they have to make their stay there more home-like. You can buy new pillowcases or use old ones that still have wear in them. Even fabric the width of a pillowcase will do. And don't forget longer ones for the moms. They are in need too.

Give: My friend takes any donations she gets and sends 50-pound bags of rice, oil, hygiene products, canned goods, and other items to help sustain the people until they can work again. Remember, the women's shelters and homeless shelters will also take food and monetary donations, as well as volunteers to help with the day-to-day tasks. In the Dominican Republic and other poverty-stricken countries, people come here for work. Their government does not have "safety nets" to help them. They often come here to work (that is how my friend met Sardi's great-grandmother). The items we send get distributed among a small group of people that help each other.

While thinking of Sardi, I began to think of my own heritage. My grandfather escaped Austria-Hungary when he began to see the signs of Communist Russia's plan to take over. If he had not been courageous enough to pick up himself and his wife and leave all that he knew behind, my life would have been a world away, and so different! I am so thankful to my courageous ancestors, and so many others that come to the USA to make a better life for their families. Yet, I cannot help but think of Sardi, and "but for the Grace of God, there go I!"

If the Lord has blessed you, if you are grateful for your brave immigrant grand or great-grand parents, why not show it in a tangible way. Maybe you can be a "Sardi's Hope" for another family.

I know there are many ways you can give to those in need. In fact, it is not hard to find some way to help someone who has no hope. I do hope you will find a way to give from your "thankful heart."

Question: Look through your closet and pantry. Is there something you have not worn in this season? Give it to someone in need. Do you have double or triple of a staple food item you're stocking up? There is someone who does not even have one. Give it to someone in need. It will come back to you when you have a need!

sing!

I will sing to the LORD all my life; I will sing praise to my God as long as I live.

Psalm 104:33 (NIV)

I hope you've seen the movie Sing! It is just a fun, uplifting, forget-your-cares kind of movie. If you haven't seen the movie, it is about a variety of talking animal who just want the opportunity to sing. A down-and-out music producer helps make their dreams come true by hosting a singing competition while attempting to revive an old theater to its former glory. Not all of the singers had the chance to be in the public eye, but they all sang when they had the opportunity to sing. Throughout the movie, everything that could go wrong for the producer did go wrong. Still, they sang! They sang while caring for their babies. They sang in the midst of relationship break-up. They sang when the theater had no money for the promised prize. They even sang when one of their dad's ended up in prison.

Have you ever noticed, when you are joyful, that singing will just flow form you even if you are not a singer in any formal kind of way? In Exodus 1:14 (NIV), Miriam and all the women sing a spontaneous song of victory after being saved and delivered out of the hands of the Egyptians. They are exuberant, and free! They are focused on God's power! They saw God in action, and they want to shout it from the roof tops.

Sometimes, we get our attitude stuck in "Eeyore" mode. You know, the donkey from *Winnie the Pooh* who was always sad and felt that nothing went right for him. We might know like that. I know a woman who was waiting in an oncologist's office for the result of a cancer update when she heard an attendant in the next cubicle begin singing a worship song. Even though my friend was waiting for some news about the progress of her cancer, when she heard the singing, her heart melted, and her spirit lifted.

What I'm going to say is so much easier for me to say than for anyone to do, yet we must. Praise the Lord at *all* times. You see, He is the God on the mountain top, giving the manna, parting the sea, healing the blind, lame, and sick. He is also the God of the valley of the shadow of death, sickness, job loss, and everything else that the world throws our way.

When Jesus puts His song in your heart, even on the worst day, deep down, you know He has your back. It will be okay, eventually. With that knowledge and peace of mind, you can always...sing!

Question: Is there a song that puts a smile in your heart every time you sing it? Sing it often!

the race of life

Therefore, since we are surrounded by such a great cloud of witnesses, let us throw off everything that hinders and the sin that so easily entangles. And let us run with perseverance the race marked out for us.

Hebrews 12:1 (NIV)

I am a person who likes to put pithy statements on the bulletin board I look at daily. You know, the ones that are brief, terse, forceful, and full of vigor and substance. Here's one of them: "Don't trip over something behind you."

This statement has helped me so many times when I want to make an excuse for my behavior.

Well, "My dad died when I was fourteen, so I didn't have a father's influence in my life." Or "I was always bullied about wearing glasses, so I feel very insecure." Or maybe "My mom had to work so she was never at any PTA meetings or virtually any other school events during the day."

For me, I always felt that I did not stand a chance for any of the prime spots in school plays or work-related favors given by teachers because I felt as if they barely knew my name. It was like I was always glossed over because none of the teachers knew my mom from any volunteer events.

While these things were all true and hard on me, even shaping who I became, it was just not acceptable for me to use them as a reason for not doing the right!

We are really running a race, a race called "life." And it's not a sprint; it's a triathlon. That means we will be running for a long time and in many different elements: physical, spiritual, and mental. While I am not a runner myself, I do know that in any activity, you want to be forward-looking. Imagine for a minute, you are running a race where you keep looking back over your shoulder to see how far the person is behind you. Your focus is split, your running speed is slowed, and your footing is unstable at best, disabled at worst. Pretty soon you will fall back as the line of "forward-thinking" people pass you right by.

In our own daily marathons of life, so many things can trip us up. However, if you set your mind on things above, if you have a plan to keep moving forward as God directs, you may not even notice the "past." I am thinking especially of the times in our lives when the Holy Spirit has prompted us to do something for God. Recently, in my own life, I was prompted to put "good news" in the newspaper. And what could be better news than the fact that Jesus died to pay the price for our sins?

So, I wrote out some scripture, a devotional, and then let it sit. I questioned myself, "Who are you that people will listen to you and read your words?" "Who are you when you did not even finish your degree in writing?" "Who are you with no big bank account to finance this endeavor?"

All these questions were quotes from my past coming back to trip me up. And for a long time, I let them! I listened to all that false narrative. It stopped me in my tracks. Along with the fact that it requires money and time to write for a newspaper, two commodities we are always short on.

But finally, I recognized it was the enemy trying to keep me from doing something that would be a potential blessing to others. The Holy Spirit reminded me that when He asks you to do something, He will also give you the provisions to do it. I then wrote up a proposal for the newspaper. I got a meeting with the Classified Ad Manager, and I was very well received. We established that every day a scripture would run in the classifieds. Additionally, once a month my devotional would run with the scripture. Behold, it was finally launched!

There's just no better feeling in the world than to be obedient to what God asks you to do. Now, I pray daily that God's Word will not return without good fruit. He established it in me; I maintain it for Him.

I think about the fact that if I had allowed those negative words in my head to keep tripping me as I looked back, this entire concept of *daily gems to spark your spirit* would not have been birthed. I do trust it is an encouragement to those who need a gentle push to get going with the idea God birthed in your heart. And isn't He speaking to all of us?

Question: Is the Holy Spirit prompting you to step out in faith with a project? If so, where? Remember, just step forward; don't look back!

who am i in Christ?

The Lord is my shepherd, I lack nothing. He makes me lie down in green pastures, he leads me beside quiet waters, he refreshes my soul. He guides me along the right paths for his name's sake. Even though I walk through the darkest valley, I will fear no evil, for you are with me; your rod and your staff, they comfort me. You prepare a table before me in the presence of my enemies. You anoint my head with oil; my cup overflows. Surely your goodness and love will follow me all the days of my life, and I will dwell in the house of the Lord forever.

Psalm 23:1-6 (NIV)

I have often been in a state of mind where I was just confused about who I was and where I was going. Maybe I was between jobs, or at a job I didn't like, and I would say, "Who am I? What am I supposed to be doing on this earth?" Maybe you have felt that way yourself sometimes.

Two brothers can be walking on a path they are not familiar with, going to a place they have never been. Yet, they are not concerned or confused. Why? Because their big, strong daddy is walking right behind them! It should be no different with us when we know Jesus as our Savior. Our "big, strong daddy," with every answer to all our questions, walks right beside us.

Here are some words from the Word that may give us some prospective. Dwell on these verses and you will find your mood improve, your prospective change, and your enthusiasm for life return. Sound like a lot from just "words?" Well, these words are not just words, God said, "in the beginning was the Word, and the Word was with God, and the Word was God" (John 1:1, NIV). There is Power in the Word of God, because the Word *is* God.

I am *blessed*: "So then those who are people of faith [whether Jew or Gentile] are blessed and favored by God [and declared free of the guilt of sin and its penalty, and placed in right standing with Him] along with Abraham, the believer" (Galatians 3:9, AMP).

I am *more than a conqueror*: "Yet in all these things we are more than conquerors and gain an overwhelming victory through Him who loved us [so much that He died for us]" (Romans 8:37, AMP).

I am *complete in Him*: "And in Him you have been made complete [achieving spiritual stature through Christ], and He is the head over all rule and authority [of every angelic and earthly power]" (Colossians 2:10, AMP).

I am *free from condemnation*: "Therefore there is now no condemnation [no guilty verdict, no punishment] for those who are in Christ Jesus [who believe in Him as personal Lord and Savior]" (Romans 8:1, AMP).

I am *His faithful follower*: "Therefore become imitators of God [copy Him and follow His example], as well-beloved children [imitate their father]" (Ephesians 5:1, AMP).

Make it your new normal to read and marinate in these words of God. I can tell you truly, you will not remain the same, you will be "new and improved."

Question: Let me ask you, once you have tried this reading experiment for a few days, what changes have you seen in your mood, behavior, or response to stress?

worry? not me

Therefore, do not worry about tomorrow, for tomorrow will worry about itself. Each day has enough trouble of its own.

Matthew 6:34 (NIV)

When I wrote this, the calendar said "Spring!" But apparently no one had notified Mother Nature because it was snowing. It was just a dusting, but since I was able to walk outside the day before, it felt like a step backward. As I was thinking about the global pandemic, yet again, I read the verse above, and I felt very positive. I was recently reminded of learning how to swim when I was a child. My mom was a great swimmer, but my dad could barely float. Obviously, it was up to Mom to teach my brother and me to swim. So, we went out to a lake. Not a nice, clean, flat bottom lake or pool for us. No, we had a muddy, uneven bottom, green-floating-stuff-water lake. You couldn't even open your eyes underwater if you wanted to because, if you dared to, you couldn't see!

I was the first to learn. After all, I was older. Mom took me in her arms and started walking out into the water. Deeper and deeper she went. She was up to her knees, then thighs, then I started feeling the cool water on my feet. I laughed because the water was tickling my feet. She kept going out farther. I felt the water on my thighs. I held on to her a little tighter, but I still grinned. She went deeper. She was chest deep. I was neck deep. I started crying and telling her to get me out! She went back into shallow water until I calmed down. Then she gave me this speech: "I am your Mother. I love you very much, and I will not allow anything harmful to happen to you! I am an expert swimmer, and I often earned medals for swimming, including as a lifeguard. I will not allow anything to happen to you."

The fear erased from my four-year-old mind. I was ready to be transported again into the deep. When she took me out there, I loosened my grip on her and relaxed. She held me under my arms and allowed me to move freely through the water as she twirled around. It was freedom! Finally, with her hands under my tummy she let me "swim" using different strokes, but I was still connected to her. Ultimately, she removed her hands without my knowledge. And, I was swimming on my own!

We know our Heavenly Father loves us so much more than even our earthly parents do. We know He is all knowing, all powerful, and everywhere at all times. Let's let go of our fear and enjoy the water!

Question: Can we ever learn how to swim if we are always safely on shore? Can we ever do anything new if we always played it safe? Ask yourself, "What have I been too scared to do?" I say to you, if God told you to do it, He will get you through it!

Worry? Not me!

aquamarine—forgiveness

be joyful, patient, prayerful, repeat!

Be joyful in hope, patient in affliction, faithful in prayer.

Romans 12:12 (NIV)

I am not one to get involved in a series when it comes to books or movies. It just seems like too long of a wait until the next one comes out, and by then, I will most likely forget the story line or have moved on to something else. However, there is one series that I really enjoy. While it came out in the '70s, I did not start watching it until recently when my grandson got me interested. It's *Star Wars*.

I have seen so many correlations between these out-of-this-world movies and God's universe, and I will address more of these as time goes on. But for today, I want to address just three words: joyful, patient, and prayerful.

The verse above reminds us that the God of this universe has a great plan for us! Think about that for a minute. If you had all the resources ever made at your fingertips, what would you do? Let your imagination go wild! Would you invent something or find the cure for a disease or plan a fabulous trip? The possibilities are endless. Often, we are content to think inside our little box of things we are so used to doing. But think BIG! We have a big God. This scripture tells us to be joyful for all God is planning. I sometimes wonder if we do not have access to His great plans because we are thinking too small. Let that marinate in your mind as you allow your thoughts to connect with God's plan.

Back to *Star Wars*. Did they have trouble? Oh yes. Were they patient? Not always. But the Lord implores us to be patient in trouble! Really? How do we do that? Well, a few years ago, I had my femur broken by a Labrador retriever. Bones take time to heal in order to be useful again. While I was healing, I wasn't capable of standing on it on my own for a long time. I had to be patient with my doctors as they inspected their work and my therapists as they instructed me how to walk again. I had to be patient with my family as I sat with my leg elevated and they did the things I wanted to do. Eventually, I was up and back to a new normal. The entire process taught me to be patient with a lot of things. Maybe, it was a lesson I needed to learn, and God knew this hard-head would not get it any other way!

The third part of this "trilogy" God gives us in this verse I did not see in *Star Wars*. There were many times the characters really should have relied on God to help, but they called on "the Force" instead. While "the Force" they call on in *Star Wars* does seem to be powerful, it is not the force that created the universe. Prayer to our creative God gives us access to power to go beyond a light saber or a spaceship.

If you watch any *Star Wars* movies, remember the force that created everything from the smallest particle to the largest lives in you in the manifest form of the Holy Spirit. No weapon formed against you will prosper with that force inside you!

Question: What part of your life right now needs the power of the Holy Spirit to intervene? Just ask for it!

Bless you

Bless those who persecute you; bless and do not curse. Rejoice with those who rejoice; mourn with those who mourn.

Romans 12:14-15 (NIV)

Have you ever tried to do this? Bless the one who is persecuting you, I mean. It's not an easy thing to do. In fact, usually we do just the opposite, but when it is done, it's a beautiful thing.

I am thinking about Betsie and Corrie ten Boom. Both were imprisoned in concentration camps for harboring Jews in their home, keeping them from death during World War II in Nazi Germany. Neither of them had to open their home as a refuge, and they were not originally sought after by the Germans. Yet this family took the second part of this verse to heart: "rejoice with those who rejoice, weep with those who weep" (Romans 12:15, NIV). They could not bear the persecution of others without easing their suffering.

While they were in the camps, Betsie was very forgiving and kind to everyone. It took Corrie a little longer, but she finally came around. Betsie died in the camp in the beginning of December 1944, but Corrie was released from Ravensbruck twelve days later. She was not scheduled to be released, but a miraculous clerical "error" worked in her favor. Corrie would often say that those who forgave their captors did much better in their lives.

She was speaking to a group once when she came face to face with one of the cruelest guards in Ravensbruck. He walked up to her after her speech on forgiveness and asked her to forgive him! She said, "For a long moment we grasped each other's hands, the former guard and the former prisoner. I had never known God's love so intensely as

I did then." It was a moment sealed in the heavens!

It is difficult to forgive. Yet, Corrie was able to forgive the person who treated her and her sister so badly. She was able to forgive even after her sister died in prison under that guard's care. When we think about the many times our great Savior has forgiven us, how can we not forgive an offense on this sin-filled earth?

Maybe you face a terrible injustice or injury. Maybe you believe you will never be able to forgive the infraction. Think of Corrie and Jesus when you are trying to forgive. Jesus told us more than once if we fail to forgive, we ourselves will not be forgiven.

Question: Have you forgiven everyone who did you wrong, hurt you, cheated you, treated you unfairly? If not, why not? Hasn't Jesus forgiven you?

Bread of Life

Everyone ought to examine themselves before they eat of the bread and drink from the cup. For those who eat and drink without discerning the body of Christ eat and drink judgment on themselves. That is why many among you are weak and sick, and a number of you have fallen asleep.

1 Corinthians 11:28-30 (NIV)

Guess what? During the global pandemic, my husband found what he was looking for in the grocery store…yeast! He immediately came back and began his bread making, and the house was filled with the yummy aroma of homemade bread.

But for now, I want to focus on these verses above. Let a man examine himself. God's Word clearly tells us that we should not expect to live our lives in a haphazard, willy-nilly manner. Each of us has been given the gift of a certain number of days on earth. What we do with them, well, that's our prerogative. Yet just like we have expectations for our children and our parents have expectations for us, our God also has expectations for us. His gifts to us are numerous, and He will never take them back.

Self-examination is a very valuable tool to check our progress toward a goal. I remember working in a marketing department making phone calls. I had a script and several benchmarks I had to meet to continue working on this project. I was always scared when the supervisor would call me to the office for my evaluation. They had an audio tape of several of my calls for us to listen to together. Those audio tapes revealed if I hit or miss the benchmarks. Way too many times I came out in tears because I had missed the mark!

In this job situation when I missed the mark, I was taken from that project and put back on the "regular calls." It stung, but after more training, I got the opportunity to try again.

Life has a set of "benchmarks" God handed down to us. He says, "regularly examine yourself." No one has a tape recording of what we did. No one will take us out of the situation and move us back a peg or two. Yet, when we don't examine ourselves and make the appropriate changes, our lives and relationships suffer! When we responded to that person rudely, when we became angry and mean when someone upset our day, when we are inconsiderate to a worker in a store or a family member, we place a smudge on the beauty of Christ's reflection.

When I was a child, I went to confession with a priest. I was always confused about what to tell him. Apparently, I didn't know the expectations God had for me well enough to search my heart for wrongdoing. Now however, I know it is expected of me to be a reflection of Jesus in what I do. I often find many flaws when I look in my mirror. When I find a flaw, I confess it and try not to do it again. Sometimes I must confess it over and over until I get it right. Yet without knowledge from the Word of what God expects of me, I would never know what I am doing wrong. Likewise, if I didn't examine myself against that standard, I would remain in my sin.

So, my husband's bread came out perfect! A comfort to my weary spirit. Yet, when I put it in my mouth, I was reminded that I cannot live on bread alone for the nourishment I need to stay healthy. And I cannot live on the "bread" of the Word to stay on the right track spiritually. I also need the convicting, exposing, harsh instruction from the Word to be able to expect to examine myself correctly. One day we will stand before a judgement seat. The events of our lives will then be played for us, similar to my audio tape at work. I don't want to leave that meeting crying! I want the Lord to say, "Welcome home, your sins are forgiven!"

Question: If you have not been examining yourself to see how you are living up to God's benchmark, will you be ready to stand at that great judgement seat?

guilty as charged!

Blessed is the one whose transgressions are forgiven; whose sins are covered. Blessed is the one whose sin the Lord does not count against them and in whose spirit is no deceit.

Psalm 32:1-2 (NIV)

It was early evening on a beautiful summer day when I was driving home on Main Avenue in our little town. I had the music blaring, the windows down, and something I was pondering filled my mind. I drove right through a recently turned red light. Though I was not aware that I did it and no one was coming the other way, a policeman, doing his sworn duty, caught me. Immediately, the lights flashed, and the siren wailed. I thought, *I better pull over; the police are after someone and need to get by me.* Then I found out it was *me* he was pulling over!

Of course, I rolled my window down the rest of the way, put my hands on the wheel, and waited. Boy, the officer took a long time getting out of the car and walking three feet to mine. Afterward, I learned during that time he was "running my plates" to gather information about me and my car. Finally, he was beside my car and asked if I knew what I did. I was not really sure, but I might have just run that red light. Bingo!

I admitted my wrongdoing, reached for the information that he asked for, and noticed his name badge.

"Are you related to Mike Martin?" I asked.

"Do you know Mike Martin?" he replied sternly.

"Yes, he goes to my church," I answered.

His face softened. "He is my brother."

"Oh, he's a good friend of mine. I probably saw you at his birthday party last year," I replied. I was not really trying to schmooze him, just being friendly.

I saw him tear the ticket and the copy for his record out of his book. Thinking it was coming to me, I put my hand out for it and said, "I am sorry officer. My mind was somewhere else. I should have been paying better attention. I intend to do so from now on."

I thought I covered all my bases and maybe he would be merciful since I had no other infractions. What he did next shocked me. He tore up the ticket. I was dumbfounded. I thought I was not reading this clearly. I hadn't been stopped by a policeman since I was identified incorrectly at age sixteen. I didn't know what to do next. He said, "You are free to go." I thanked him.

I drove the three blocks to my home, shaking while the weight of that encounter sunk in. I was guilty. I was going to receive the pronouncement of my deserved punishment. I said one name. I was free!

Do you see the significance of this encounter? The next day I sat with paper and pen. I wrote a beautiful letter to the officer explaining that what he did for me was what Jesus did for all of us when He took the cross for my guilt.

I never heard what happened when the officer received the letter. In fact, I even lost track of Mike. But I know this, God's Word does not go forth without producing fruit. Maybe at some point the policeman will be in a hard spot and remember the woman who deserved a ticket but did not get one and what that meant in the spiritual world.

Here's a thought for you: In our day-to-day world, it's sometimes difficult to find the right opportunity to share Jesus with people. However, sometimes the Lord allows events to occur so that the opportunity is facing us. What do we do with it? First, we need to have our eyes open to the opportunity. Second, we need to take full advantage of it. That may be the only opportunity that person will hear the clear message of the gospel. Make sure you are prepared to give it. It's as simple as "ABC."

> A: Admit you have sinned. "If we claim to be without sin, we deceive ourselves and the truth is not in us" (1 John 1:8, NIV).
>
> B: Believe in the Savior. "For God so loved the world that he gave his one and only Son, that whoever believes in him shall not perish but have eternal life" (John 3:16, NIV).
>
> C: Confess and forsake your sin. "If we confess our sins, he is faithful and just and will forgive us our sins and purify us from all unrighteousness" (1 John 1:9, NIV).

Question: Do you have your spiritual "radar" tuned into the opportunities the Lord places before you regularly? Do you take advantage of them?

improve your smile!

All Scripture is God-breathed and is useful for teaching, rebuking, correcting and training in righteousness.

2 Timothy 3:16 (NIV)

I was just amazed at the amount of drilling going on today! First, it started in one area, then before I knew it there were two professionals with the drills and other equipment working on a second and even a third area. The noise was deafening, and the debris was flying. It was so close to my head! I was in the middle of it all. I was getting crowns on three teeth.

Of course, after three shots of the numbing medication, I was feeling no pain. My mind was racing, however, as the dentist and the dental technician hovered over me. I felt like a road, and they were the construction workers.

I had a lot of time to think when I was incapacitated with equipment and goop in my mouth, not to mention the drillers over my face. Four minutes later and a mold was made and hardened. I just closed my eyes and allowed the Holy Spirit to speak, listening for the dentist's instructions too: "Open wide," "Bite down," "Grind a little." I'll admit, I had to be told twice a couple times as I was not paying attention.

When I got back to what the Holy Spirit was saying, I was fascinated. He was talking about the drilling process. It was an amazing, high-tech way of fixing my teeth, yet the process is replicated in our lives daily. We are similar to a mouth full of teeth with cavities. Daily, the garbage we watch, read, listen to, and even think of gives us rotten "cavities" of stuff in our lives. Things we see spur emotions that lead to speech, and then action. These rotten things need to be "drilled out" before they hit the nerve. If the nerve is hit, an entirely different procedure must ensue. Root Canal. This is a much more extensive and painful way to get the rotten, diseased parts out before replacing it with good material. But it can be done, and the Holy Spirit is capable of doing it. There is one caveat to this entire improvement project: we must say "yes" to it. My teeth had been in disrepair for quite a while. It wasn't until I was motivated to begin the process of repair that the repair could begin. The beauty at the end of this process is that I will have some beautiful, fully functional teeth with no more pain.

Same with us. We may see the rot or sin in our lives. We may know in our heads it does us no good to have it there. However, it's not until we are convicted by the Holy Spirit to remove it that we begin the painful process of drilling or even a root canal. The beauty of this process is we will have a restored inner beauty. We will be able to function in truth, no more secrets, and the pain of being hypocritical in some areas of our lives will be eliminated. Another very special part of the process is that we have the promise that the Lord will walk with us through it. Though He does not take all the pain away, He does numb it enough to be bearable.

Question: At some time or another you may find yourself in the dentist chair facing that drill. Think of it as a reminder: What do I need to get drilled out of my life? Improve your smile!

judge and jury

In the presence of God and of Christ Jesus, who will judge the living and the dead, and in view of his appearing and his kingdom, I give you this charge: Preach the word; be prepared in season and out of season; correct, rebuke and encourage-with great patience and careful instruction.

2 Timothy 4:1-2 (NIV)

I have been on jury trials multiple times. While many, if not most, people don't like to be called for jury duty, I really enjoy it. Seeing the whole legal process at work and close up was so educational for me. I guess the time off work, maybe the drive, and of course the loss of your regular pay in exchange for the minimal pay a juror receives, are probably factors for not wanting to be chosen.

In the judicial process, there is a judge. He is really the referee in the courtroom. While the jury hears the evidence of the case before the court, the judge also charges the jury with the heavy weight of making the correct verdict. The judge makes it clear, in the jury instructions, that this decision is placed on the shoulders of twelve human beings.

Still, in this life, we are not the judge or jury with our peers. Only God is. He is judge and jury, the One who sees all the evidence and decides the outcome.

We have, however, been given many jobs to do by the Lord. I call them "preach, point, and push." In today's scripture passage, the Apostle Paul is telling Timothy, and ultimately us, what we need to do until the "Judge" returns. So, let's take a look at our job description. We have been told to "preach the word, reprove, rebuke and exhort" (2 Timothy 4:2, NIV). And we need to do all that with "great patience and careful instruction" (2 Timothy 4:2, NIV).

I'm just going to say this first off. Not all of us will preach from a pulpit. But we will still preach! My husband was a pastor of a church that decreased to about twenty people before we were assigned there. When we retired, it was up to about 200. Was that my husband's doing? Only in the sense that he did what he was told by the Holy Spirit.

Now scripture tells the pastor of any church to "equip" the saints. Once the people have the knowledge, they go out and "preach" without even speaking a word. In all of our actions, interactions, responses, and behaviors, we are preaching! Perhaps you've heard the age-old saying, "I preach the gospel every day. Sometimes, I use words!"

I remember one job I had as office manager of a home health agency for the elderly. The other woman in the office was very high strung. One day when I returned after a day off, she said, "You cannot take any time off again. The office was in chaos! But as soon as you walk in, the office is calm."

I didn't know what to make of that statement, but later the Holy Spirit reminded me, "When you walked in, I did too." And the Holy Spirit, part of the Godhead, carries a peace that passes all understanding. My husband had similar experiences when he was a teacher. When he was in the classroom, things ran smoothly. The other teachers would tell him of the upheavals when he was not there. That's how we preach! And those experiences give us the opportunities to explain the "hope" that lies within us.

We have also been given instructions to "reprove and rebuke" when we see people starting down the wrong path. This one is much harder to do because it's not always received well. It is their choice, for their own good. Yet, if they are not aware of this scripture verse, they may think you are out of line.

Here are two experiences I have had with reproving and rebuking with two different outcomes: We have seen couples living together without the blessing of marriage on their lives. After explaining to one couple that God cannot bless them "abundantly" without being under His covenant umbrella, they got married. Their lives were immediately free from the guilt and bondage of sin, and they began to flourish. On the other hand, the other couple continued to delay the marriage citing "money" as their reasoning for the delay. Since the cost of a marriage license is reasonably affordable, "money" was not a good excuse. Their lives have continued to roll along like a car on a pothole-ridden road, bumpy and rough to say the least. God just cannot go against His Word and bless sin.

I am also reminded that we have a responsibility to gently point to something that needs attention in a friend's life. We can be held accountable if we don't. Let's say, gossip. Put up a "stop sign" when friends begin to gossip. As difficult as it may seem, you are making them aware of something they may not have noticed since it had become such a habit. If nothing else, they will probably think twice before sharing some gossip with you.

The last job we have is finishing what we started. Once we have pointed to the sin, now we can point to the way that will bring peace and prosperity. Exhortation is the ability to give a little push in the right direction to people who have expressed their need to change. You may do this by encouraging them to join a Bible study or teach a Bible study. Maybe it's to lead a group or just go to one. Whatever it may be, we must use great patience and instruction when we exhort people. Case in point: I am very new to writing so my dear friend came alongside me and patiently instructed me, for hours! That's an exhorter extraordinaire!

So, watch how you are living your life. Are you preaching a sermon that will expose a person's sin and push them onto the right path? Or is your life preaching a sermon that is somewhat less than it should be? You will be preaching, no matter what!

Question: Can you remember a time in your life when you gently gave a little push in the right direction to someone who needed it? How did that turn out?

let's run!

Peace I leave with you; my peace I give you. I do not give to you as the world gives. Do not let your hearts be troubled and do not be afraid.

John 14:27 (NIV)

In late spring 2020, I felt something in the air! We had been in the midst of the global pandemic and mostly at home for months, but that day, as we drove to bring my mom her Sunday dinner, there were many more cars on the road than I had seen out before. A few days later, when we went to a fabric store, I was pleasantly surprised to find many cars in the lot and many people in the store. When I talked to my neighbor days after, he was excited to be planting his raised garden soon. My neighbor on the other side said his by-appointment-only business was picking up. I believe what I was feeling was optimism! Yes, I know it was. I thought we were seeing the light at the end of this long tunnel of COVID-19 getting brighter. We had been doing all the restrictive things we had been asked to do. We had endured the hardship of distancing from family. We had watched every Hallmark movie we ever wanted to see, read every book we never had time to read, tried new recipes, and even caught up on extra cleaning! We were ready! Well, almost.

I want you to think about a group of runners at the starting line. They are ready. Their training, exercising, practicing is finished. They need one last thing, like we do: mental preparedness. They need to make up their mind to finish the run no matter what happens along the way. We need that focus as well!

During the pandemic, I have made some improvements in my daily time with the Lord. Of course, I spent more time reading and praying since I had the time. I also began focusing my prayers. While our prayers are never wasted, just like the focused runner, a focused prayer has a much better chance of being effectual.

Let's just focus on the verse above. The Lord is telling us He is leaving peace with us, one of the gifts He gives us in Galatians 5:22 (NIV). When He gives His gifts, He does not take them back. So, I am pretty certain that we can conclude that we *have* peace! He even says, "Peace I leave with you; my peace I give you. I do not give to you as the world gives" (John 14:27, NIV). We know we can feel peaceful when things are going well, bills are paid, we have a job and our health, but that is the peace the world gives. That peace can disappear quickly when we are faced with a pandemic. No, God's peace goes far beyond the world's peace. It is "the peace of God, which transcends all understanding" (Philippians 4:7, NIV) It is the peace you can believe in when we are faced with a crisis, cancer, job loss, death of a loved one, uncertain economy. It is the peace that says, "I've got the whole world in my hands, and I'm not going to drop it!" Just let that peace sink in for a minute.

So really, when we have Jesus in our hearts, He walks with us daily. We have the assurance that if we continue to live here on earth, or if He takes us home to Heaven, we are in His care. Now that's peace!

Question: Do you have that peace? Since it's a gift for us all, just ask for it!

live at peace with everyone

Now the LORD is the Spirit, and where the Spirit of the LORD is, there is freedom. And we all, who with unveiled faces contemplate the LORD's glory, are being transformed into his image with ever-increasing glory, which comes from the LORD, who is the Spirit.

2 Corinthians 3:17-18 (NIV)

Ever wonder how children learn so quickly? I watch as my out-of-town grandchildren especially seem to grow in knowledge at twice the rate of speed that I did.

My granddaughter just graduated from high school and already has a plethora of knowledge in her pretty head that I did not acquire until much later in my life. My grandson is going into middle school. He is mesmerized by rocket launches and loves science experiments. Maybe a future astronaut in our family?

Many generations of people have gained their knowledge from reading the Bible. As we have read it over so many years, our information has increased. Our wisdom has increased, and we are a more productive people.

When we walk with the Lord, we study His Word, listen to His Word, live out His Word, we cannot help but gain knowledge and a thirst for more knowledge. The world is fascinating and finding out more about the world is invigorating. As people who study the Word, we have an advantage over those who don't. How so? Well, many phrases come from the Bible. You would not know that if you didn't read it. Many science and geography references become part of our vocabulary and knowledge we draw on, some of which are only learned from experience and not from school. There are many references to behavior and how to reduce anxiety that are very beneficial to keep us emotionally healthy. Much of Psalms and Proverbs teach us ways to live peacefully, legally, and even free from marriage problems. It's like free counseling!

This scripture is telling us when we have a face-to-face relationship with the Lord, we are changed, invigorated, transformed from one level of information to a higher level. As we continue to know Him better, we continue to grow in knowledge and life skills that keep us healthy, happy, and wise. And you just thought the Bible was a spiritual book!

Question: What have you learned from the Bible that helped you in life that was not spiritual in nature?

queen esther in lancaster county

When Esther's words were reported to Mordecai, he sent back this answer: "Do not think that because you are in the king's house you alone of all the Jews will escape. For if you remain silent at this time, relief and deliverance for the Jews will arise from another place, but you and your father's family will perish. And who knows but that you have come to your royal position for such a time as this?"

Esther 4:12-14 (NIV)

If you have never taken a trip to the Sight and Sound Theater in Lancaster County, PA, you are missing something so amazing Hollywood would be envious! Aside from the fact that the music is all original, the sets and costumes are out of this world, and every actor does a phenomenal job, no matter what the performance, the Biblical truths the actors make come alive are life changing. Please go see it!

This particular book in the Bible, Esther, has always been a favorite of mine. A young girl "rags to riches" story. Every girl's dream is to become a queen and wear beautiful clothes. I have read the story many times, but I did not see the agony of the young girl, Hadassah, until I saw it play out on the stage.

Hadassah was an orphan raised by her relative, Mordecai. Their people were exiled to Persia many generations before and they lived a peaceful life in Persia as devout Jews. Then suddenly, their world turned upside down as the non-submissive Queen Vashti was dismissed, and a new queen had to be found for King Xerxes. A call went out to the young beautiful women in Sousa, Persia to be brought in before the king after a time of pampering. Hadassah was chosen! Her name was changed to Esther by her uncle to protect her Jewish heritage from discovery.

Through a series of events, the king's advisor, Haman, betrayed the Jewish remnant in Sousa. After the plot was exposed, the king ordered Haman to be hung on the gallows, and Mordecai, who exposed the plot, was honored.

The entire story reads like a novel of intrigue, but the underlying story is just as pertinent to us today as it was to the Jews in 479 B.C. Let's unpack the story:

There are five main characters in the story who reveal to us that currents events are only a repeat of ancient events.

First, Queen Vashti. She was not about to obey the king to parade in front of his drunk buddies at a banquet that had been going on for 180 days! As a result, he had her deposed as queen.

Second, King Xerxes. His father was a king and had been tolerant, if not kind, to the Jews living in his province of Persia after they were exiled from Jerusalem.

Third, Haman, the king's advisor. He had a dislike, well a hate, for Mordecai because Mordecai refused bow to Haman as the law stated. As a result, Haman wanted Mordecai hung on the gallows and then wanted the entire tribe of the Jews killed.

Fourth, Mordecai, a relative of Hadassah who raised her and now watched at the King's gate to be near her if she needed him.

Finally, Hadassah, a beautiful and devout Jewish orphan, when the story begins; Esther, a powerful and brave woman who saves the Jewish remnant at the end of the story. She realizes she might be the only way her people would survive and concludes, "if I perish, I perish."

Connections to today: We are in an age when our very core is being torn at and everything, we, as Judeo-Christians, stand for is being pulled down. Laws are being made that are diabolical, yet, when we cannot agree or obey, we suffer consequences.

Yet, there is a remnant of Godly believers who are standing up for what is right. We are praying and having our own "protests" by standing up for ourselves. Esther and Mordecai knew God was the only solution to their problem, and they had been chosen to stand for their people.

God always makes a way! That's the good news. He had the plan all along to rescue His people from the hands of the enemy. He already has the plan and has people in place, and we just continue to pray and wait until we see His hand move in our nation. In Esther's case, she was the beloved queen of Xerxes who saved him from a death threat and her people from annihilation. Mordecai was elevated in the Persian government to second in command, and all of the Jews throughout Persia were also treated with respect.

"Lord, please work your will and way in this nation that has its heritage in You and Your Word, Amen."

Question: Is there a line you will not cross if asked to do so, even by your government? How will you respond when there are consequences to disobey?

healing through the ten commandments

If my people, who are called by my name, will humble themselves and pray and seek my face and turn from their wicked ways, then I will hear from heaven, and I will forgive their sin and will heal their land.

2 Chronicles 7:14 (NIV)

Oftentimes, it can be quite beneficial to methodically study each individual part of a scripture, like the one for today.

So, here comes the hard part of this promise God gives us: we need to turn from our wicked ways! Yes, us, those of us who call ourselves Christians. The verse says, "people called by my name" (2 Chronicles 7:14, NIV). We don't like to do that. We are like spoiled children who want our own way no matter what our parent says!

But how do we know what a "wicked way" is? Well, for starters, let's look at the Ten Commandments. They have been the benchmark in our society since the beginning of our nation. They have been permanently inscribed on government buildings in many states and Washington D.C. And they are as pertinent today as they were back when Moses brought them down from the mountain in Exodus 20:1-17 (NIV) and Deuteronomy 5:6-21 (NIV). They have not changed with the trends, they have not lost their power, and they still keep our society on an even keel and align with what is best for us.

Ten Commandments

You shall have no other gods before Me.

You shall make no idols.

You shall not take the name of the Lord your God in vain.

Keep the Sabbath day holy.

Honor your father and your mother.

You shall not murder.

You shall not commit adultery.

You shall not steal.

You shall not bear false witness against your neighbor.

You shall not covet.

When we break one of these, we break them all. So, we may try to justify our bad behavior by saying we have not murdered. But I am sure we all have lied. Have you wanted something someone else has? Have you talked back to your parents? If you've done any of these, then you've broken them all. You get my point. There is no way, in our natural self, that we could keep all ten of the commandments, all the time. Only Jesus was able to do that. Thank You, Jesus, You came so we would have forgiveness and the promise of heaven.

God gave us His solution to our sinful ways, and God's promise remains: *if* people who call themselves believers will cry out to Him, He *will* hear us from His home in Heaven. He *will* forgive our sins, and He *will* heal our land. People, we need a literal healing in our land right now! Let's make a conscious effort daily to turn from our wicked ways and ask for His forgiveness. There is still hope in our God and a promise we can count on!

Question: Do you still believe in the Ten Commandments or do you believe they have become irrelevant for today? Remember, God's Word does not change! We must change to align with His standards. It's the only way.

diamond—home

a party invitation

Do not let your hearts be troubled. You believe in God; believe also in me. My Father's house has many rooms; if that were not so, would I have told you that I am going there to prepare a place for you? And if I go and prepare a place for you, I will come back and take you to be with me that you also may be where I am.

John 14:1-3 (NIV)

Recently, I received an invitation to a party. I was so excited to go because it was at a very well known, posh place I had never been before. The invitation was from one of my best friends so I knew I would have a great time. The only problem was that the restaurant was not very big, and everyone I talked to about it also got an invitation.

I began to wonder then worry: would there be enough room? I get really uncomfortable at parties that are wall-to-wall people. I thought, *Maybe I won't go. If I were to go, would I even see the host?* I had been to events before where I was squeezing past people holding their food and beverage, and so was I. Inevitably someone's drink sloshes on you. *No, I won't go*, I thought, *But it is a beautiful place, and I do really like the people who invited me.* I decided to go, but that meant the parking lot would be packed too. I also don't like arriving an hour early just to get a parking spot. I decided I wouldn't go.

Maybe you have had a similar debate with yourself about something you have been invited to. But just think, would the host really invite so many people that you would be squished? Would the fire marshal even allow that? In today's scripture verse, Jesus is talking about a home He is preparing for us to dwell in for eternity, once we get to Heaven. He is working on it even now, and I am sure since

He rules the universe, there will be enough room for everyone who professes Jesus as their Lord and Savior.

So, I decided to go to the party, and I am so glad I did! The venue had such a surge in their business that they expanded the hall and the parking. I had a blast, the food was great, and my host took time to chat, (and even dance) with me!

Remember, this earth is *not* our permanent residence. Be sure you have sent back your heavenly RSVP. You are not going to want to miss this party!

Read Revelation 21 (NIV) for further details on the "room" Jesus is preparing for us.

Question: Have you ever wondered what your heavenly home (mansion) is going to look like? You might want to write out a description.

are we there yet?

Jesus answered, "I am the way and the truth and the life. No one comes to the Father except through me."

John 14:6 (NIV)

If you have ever taken a road trip with kids (or been a kid yourself on a road trip), you have heard this question expressed, "Are we there yet?" When the answer is not suitable, a deep groan usually ensues. We like to be where we planned to go!

A few years ago, I took my two grandchildren on a trip to a park we had never been to before. It was a beautiful summer day, I had my GPS system loaded with the address, we had water and snacks, and we were off! After the time allotted by the navigation system, it said, "You have reached your destination." I stopped the car and looked around. My grandson was exasperated and said, "Nana, you brought us to a cemetery?" I was looking at it too, an old, run-down cemetery with flags flying over a few old graves. It was not what we were expecting at all.

I looked at the GPS, at the address, and back again at the cemetery. What happened? This is not where we were supposed to be going.

Well, I still don't know exactly what happened with my GPS. I was a little confused. I had a choice to make as I stared at the tombstones: turn around and go home or continue to search for my planned destination. I was able to re-trace my directions, and finally we found what we were looking for and much more! The park was beautiful, well maintained, and we had a wonderful day. I made the right choice.

Experts tell us that the thought of the destination you envision in your mind is the motivation to keep on going when the path you have chosen seems out of reach or too difficult to get to.

Many people have gone through the most horrific situations against their will and survived by keeping a vision of their future success in their mind's eye. Holocaust victims, prisoners of war, and victims of crimes all keep hope alive in their hearts by envisioning their future free and whole.

We will have an ultimate destination when our physical bodies run out of strength for life. There are only two choices we can enter into our eternal "GPS" system: heaven or hell. God made it so easy to enter Heaven into the system: choose Jesus. However, if we fail to choose because we cannot decide, we have inadvertently made the decision for hell. Since no one knows when the time of our death will happen, it's best to be ready.

Set your GPS with your choice today while you can. One thing I will say, you can trust God's providential system. He sent someone who took our place when a price had to be paid for our wrongs against God. We will ultimately end up at a cemetery, but only our physical body. Our eternal body will be at the glorious new destination: heaven.

My husband recently officiated a funeral of some dear friends' mom. He was able to tell the family, with assurance, she chose heaven as she told my husband she made that choice.

Question: Have you set your GPS system for heaven? Remember the default is hell. Make the decision today.

are you contaminated?

> Therefore, since we have these promises, dear friends, let us purify ourselves from everything that contaminates body and spirit, perfecting holiness out of reverence for God.
>
> 2 Corinthians 7:1 (NIV)

During the pandemic, we knew that we had an invisible enemy lurking everywhere! We also knew that we would be able to get back to our normal lives eventually. But at that point would we really be contaminant free? Oh sure, our hands and surfaces would be clean and sanitized. We would be much more careful about touching our surroundings and faces. Yet, none of those contaminants have the power that one contaminant has. Oh, it is often invisible, but there is no amount of hand sanitizer or bleach that will rid you of this contaminant. Its name is sin.

Sin was the problem that got Adam and Eve kicked out of the Garden of Eden never to return. Their perfect world shattered for a bite of fruit. Sin is the invisible culprit that will break up marriages, give us depression, drive us to alcoholism, drug use, theft, homelessness, and more because we have no hope. Sin is responsible for all of the terror, financial woes, and, often, the general lethargy we feel about life.

What is the medicine that can combat this awful virus? There is only one: salvation through Jesus Christ. When I was a teenager, I first heard the term "saved." I kept asking, "Saved? Saved from what?" Finally, a friend took me to the church he went to, and I heard the whole story about the gospel of Jesus right from the Bible. I went to church every Sunday until I was fourteen-years-old, but I never heard the "good news" that Jesus saves. During my teen years, many of my loved ones died. Their funerals were all in churches. Yet, I never heard the "good news" about Jesus. I did stop going to church for two years. I was not asked about, called, or visited by a priest who could tell me about the love of Jesus. I was lost! I didn't know my purpose in this life. I had very little self-worth and no direction in life. I was at a crossroad that could have gone very badly, but God intervened.

For the first time in forever, I heard what I needed to be saved from: hell. I heard that sin is a great chasm that separates God from man. Jesus Christ laid His life down on the cross to become the bridge between God and man. While it is for every man and woman, we need to make the choice to accept the beautiful gift He provided for us the way to the Father God.

Once I heard this good news, I knew that was what I wanted and needed. I asked Jesus to forgive me of my sins and guide and direct my life. I now have the Holy Spirit within me, comforting and guiding me. I was never the same! All my old insecurities vanished, I became a new creation, and I never looked back. There is nothing in my old life I would want to return to.

Well, that's my story. You may have your own story about what God did in your life. I would love to hear it. If you don't have a salvation story, it's easy to get one! Easy as ABC! A: accept what Jesus did for you on the cross. B: believe He took your sins as His own. C: confess your sins to Him and ask for His forgiveness. Now you are saved from the pit of hell and on your way to heaven! Hallelujah!

If you just made this confession of faith, let me know. I would love to pray for you in your new life in Christ.

Question: If you were to die today, where would your soul be resting for eternity: heaven or hell?

do you believe this?

And whoever lives by believing in me will never die. Do you believe this?

John 11:26 (NIV)

Kind of an unusual question don't you think? Jesus is asking his friend Martha this question after her brother died. Here's what happened. The disciples and Jesus were ministering to people when they received word that a good friend of Jesus named Lazarus was sick. Lazarus had two sisters who loved him very much. One was Martha, and the other was Mary, the same Mary that anointed the feet of Jesus with expensive perfume and dried his feet with her hair. She had been healed by Jesus, and she loved Jesus. Jesus loved the three of them, so when he received word that his friend Lazarus was sick, he said, "this is a sickness not unto death, but for the glory of God that the Son of God may be glorified through it" (John 11:14, NIV). He stayed where they were two more days before leaving to go to see Lazarus in Bethany.

When Martha heard that Jesus was coming, and in fact was nearby, she ran out to meet him. She was crying and said "Lord, if you had been here my brother would not have died. But even now I know that whatever you ask of God, God will give you." Jesus told her "Your brother will rise again." She said, "I know my brother will rise again in the resurrection at the last day."

Then Jesus, in John 11:25 (NKJV), tells Martha something so beautiful that we quote this, memorize it, and take much comfort in it; Jesus says, "I am the resurrection and the life. He who believes in Me, though he may die, he shall live. And whoever lives and believes in Me shall never die. Do you believe this?" (John 11:25, NKJV).

daily gems to spark your spirit

She said, "Yes!" Martha left room in her heart for the possibility that something out of the natural realm we know, could happen. And it did!

That's when God does His best work. When we believe God can reach into our world, and for a moment in time, break the reality we are accustomed to, He can do something we call "miraculous."

Jesus stood in front of a tomb and cried out, "Lazarus, come forth!" (John 11:43, NKJV). Some say Jesus had to call specifically for Lazarus because if he said a random, "come forth," all the dead would have come out of their graves. When Jesus speaks, even the dead listen!

When he had said this, Jesus called in a loud voice, "Lazarus, come out!" (Johns 11:43, NIV). Lazarus walked out of the grave four days after he had died!

Do you believe this? This is the same thing that Jesus does in our lives when we ask him to forgive our sins and take over as Lord. He calls our name to "come forth" from that life of sin and be born again! And we come out of that muck and mire and toss off those grave clothes, becoming a new creation. And we feel all brand new. Hallelujah!

Question: Do you remember how you felt coming out of that "grave." If you cannot recall that moment, you might want to ask yourself, "Am I still in that grave?"

guardians of the force

What I am saying is that as long as an heir is underage, he is no different from a slave, although he owns the whole estate. The heir is subject to guardians and trustees until the time set by his father. So also, when we were underage, we were in slavery under the elemental spiritual forces of the world. But when the set time had fully come, God sent his Son, born of a woman, born under the law, to redeem those under the law, that we might receive adoption to sonship.

Galatians 4:1-5 (NIV)

It's almost six years ago now. Hard to even imagine life before our Preston Ronald, our youngest grandson, came on the scene. He is our last grandchild and has my husband's name for his middle name. He was a perfect baby! An almost eleven-pound perfect baby! I went to the Philadelphia area to our son and daughter-in-love's home to help care for their older child, Grant William. He was only older by twenty months. It was a happy and busy event, so it was helpful that this was a home with a "guardian" either at the door or under the bassinet 24/7! The guardian was their pit bull, Jeffrey.

Jeffery is a seventy-five-pound pit bull mix rescue dog. He became attached very quickly to me and the family. As soon as I entered the home and greeted everyone, I sat on the couch and called Jeffrey, "Come give Nana some sugar." Immediately Jeffrey came running, climbed up on my lap, and just cozied up until he had enough. Then he jumped down and returned to his post at the window or door. When Preston was in the bassinet, Jeffrey laid under it. If you thought he was asleep, you were wrong! As soon as baby Preston made a move or a squeak, Jeffery was at attention, surveying the situation. On one of these occasions when Preston continued to cry, Jeffery found the adult in the house and barked at me until I went to Preston and resolved his issue. Preston's older brother was on high alert also. If Grant was out somewhere with his Daddy, as soon as he entered the house, his twenty-month-old little frame ran to the bassinet to check on his "brudder." These two were the "guardians of the force." The "force" in that home, at that time, was Preston. He was incapable of caring for himself and needed guardians. He is still the force in that home today, and we love him dearly.

From God's vantage point, we are the "force" that needs the guardian. We are just humans, frail, and, often, incapable of knowing right from wrong! In fact, how can anyone really know right from wrong if someone does not tell us first? That is where "The Law" comes in. Before Christ came to earth, Moses was given The Law, the Ten Commandments. For years, we had The Law to keep us on the straight and narrow. The Law did a good job, for the most part, but the Word told us something better was coming. The Law was the down payment, or the security for a better plan God already had in place. We were all like the under-aged heirs of an immense fortune. We knew the fortune was coming; it had been promised by God in Isaiah 7:14. It was just a matter of God's timing when the promise will be fulfilled. "Therefore the LORD himself will give you a sign: The virgin will conceive and give birth to a son, and will call him Immanuel" (Isaiah 7:14, NIV).

Though we did not know exactly when it would come or how it would come, we did know we would receive it. Just like an inheritance: however, we could not receive what was promised until the guarantor died. That's just the way an inheritance worked. That was the only way to receive this indescribable gift from Father God. Jesus had to die!

When it all began to unfold with the birth of Jesus in Bethlehem, very few of the educated Jewish leaders were able to put the pieces of the puzzle together. There was just too much emotional attachment to this man: Jesus the healer. Not unlike ourselves when a person close to us dies, the inheritance is not our first concern. However, when the truth that the law was now exchanged for Grace and rules were now written on our hearts, our eyes were opened to salvation through the Messiah. This is what the prophet was talking about. Now, we experience it with our own eyes and understanding. Hallelujah!

It says in Galatians 3:13 (NIV), "Christ redeemed us from the curse of the law by becoming a curse for us, for it is written: 'Cursed is everyone who is hung on a pole.'"

To me it sometimes seems too good to be true. The Creator of the universe loved His creation so much that when we were so sinful, He still had a plan to redeem us back to Himself. Some things in life need to be believed to be seen.

Question: Is your inheritance in Christ secured by His death, in your heart? If not, find out how to be sure in the "Afterword" of this book.

he is risen! just as he said.

Now if we are children, then we are heirs-heirs of God and co-heirs with Christ, if indeed we share in his sufferings in order that we may also share in his glory.

Romans 8:17 (NIV)

Easter of 2020, I took some time to reflect on Easters in my past. I remember, as a school-girl, my mom getting my brother and me ready for "the" day. First, she would make me a beautiful new dress. She made most of my clothes at the time. Then we would go shopping for the accessories to match: a straw brimmed hat or a pill box hat, matching small purse, white gloves, and of course white patent leather shoes! Easter was the first day of the year we were allowed to wear white, and we did. My brother looked sharp too. He also had a hat, a suit, and new shoes.

Once we were all put together on the morning of Easter, we were off to church. Church in the Greek Catholic tradition was very different. I loved to walk in with the scent of lilies and hyacinth nearly overpowering the sanctuary. The cross was draped in purple, and His crown was on the top, but He was not there! He had risen indeed! Since most of the Mass was in Russian, I really did not grasp the significance of what the priest was saying, but I knew something very significant happened on that day. At home, we were finally able to see our simple baskets of candy. Our dinner represented elements you might see at a Passover Seder but with Christian significance: red beets with horseradish to represent the bitter experience Jesus went through, the unleavened bread to represent our sinless Savior with the yeast representing sin, and a milk and egg "cheese" ball, but I was never sure what that represented.

I enjoyed the "look back," but I could not stay there. I thought about what the resurrection meant for us beside the fact that Jesus took our sins, past, present, and future, on Him. I thought about when my mother-in-law passed away. The executor of the will, my brother-in-law, read her will. Now, we all knew she had a will; we were even aware of some of our inheritance in the will. Still, we were not able to take possession of those items until she died.

This same Jesus left an inheritance for us! The Bible is His last will and testament. Reading the "will" lets us know what we have inherited on this resurrection day. It is all we will ever need. Let's look at some of the attributes we inherited on resurrection day.

First and foremost, we become children of God. 1 Peter 1:23 (NIV) tells us if we choose to, we can be born again of incorruptible seed of the Word of God. We are the children of a King! King's kids have all they need because their father has all he needs and shares freely with the children he adores.

Second, we have total forgiveness of our sin. Our sins were washed white when we asked Jesus to wash us clean with the blood he already shed for us. Does it give us the right to go back to our sin? No! We must repent, turn from sin, and not go back to it.

Third, we can become a new creation! 2 Corinthians 6:19 (NIV) tells us out old nature is gone and we are brand new. I experienced this when I gave my heart to God. I had no direction; I was often moody and miserable. Christ entered my heart and did a remodel. I became "new and improved." Believe me, my family noticed it too.

Fourth, we are blessed! Galatians 3:9 (NIV) tells us "those who rely on faith are blessed." Blessed is a word that means made holy or consecrated. Being holy and consecrated you are set apart from the crowd because you have a higher purpose. You represent God.

Fifth, we are victorious! "Those who are victorious will inherit all this, and I will be their God and they will be my children" (Revelation 21:7, NIV).

I only gave you five of the many of attributes we inherit as God's children. I highly recommend that we dwell on these words, and they will change the way we think and even the way we believe and behave.

Question: How would my life be different if I meditated on the positive words of God?

hello march!

However, as it is written: "What no eye has seen, what no ear has heard, and what no human mind has conceived"- the things God has prepared for those who love him.

2 Corinthians 2:9 (NIV)

March. It can be such a volatile month for the weather. So much so that March has a phrase to describe it. Perhaps you've heard the old adage: "March comes in like a lion and goes out like a lamb."

We know that a lion, king of the beasts, can have power beyond compare, while the precious little lamb represents everything tame and innocent. If you saw a lion just laying down in a sunny field near you while a lamb playfully skipped around him, you would begin to wonder just how long that lazy lion will put up with that before making a lamb lunch for himself.

Yet, in a universe created by God and described in Revelation 21, God describes the "New Jerusalem." It's a place where the lion and lamb will live in peace together because that is the way God always intended it to be, even before Adam and Eve disobeyed God.

But here's something to look forward to: God will do it again! I don't know about you, but I am looking forward to running through a field with a cougar and black bear running right alongside me! Psalm 4:8 (NIV) gives us assurance we will dwell in safety, and in Isaiah 11:6 (NIV) it says, "The wolf will live with the lamb, the leopard will lie down with the goat, the calf and the lion and the yearling together; and a little child will lead them."

Wow. Imagine that beautiful and peaceful scene. According to our scripture verse for today, our human minds cannot even begin to

daily gems to spark your spirit

conceive all the awesome things God has prepared for us.

In March, the month of unpredictable weather patterns, one thing is certain: God does have a beautiful new creation planned for us!

Question: What excites you most as you ponder the New Jerusalem?

is this the end?

And this gospel of the kingdom will be preached in the whole world as a testimony to all nations, and then the end will come.

Matthew 24:14 14 (NIV)

If you have been involved in conversations recently, you have probably heard this question: "Do you think this is the end?"

So many questions arise after that question, many have no answers, many have answers, but many answers may not be a comfort if you are not ready for the end.

I write regularly to a prisoner. She has been telling me that the women there are questioning whether the events going on in the world in 2020 were the beginning of the end of the world. This gives my friend a unique opportunity. It gives us one as well!

The Bible has some very clear answers, and there are very specific things that need to happen before the end would come. There are also a couple things we can do to get ready.

Vacation season is just around the corner. Think about it, would you just pack up a bag and hop in the car going to, let's say, the airport without a plan? Would you even drive to a destination you have been to before without checking to see if they are open? I think not! So, I ask, why would you just recklessly live your life without a planned destination, after your life here expires?

Now, I don't mean a prepaid plan at a local cemetery or crematoria. I mean a plan for your eternal destination! And this plan is easy, and free!

So, first let's look at the signs to look for that signal the end of the age.

In Matthew 24: 3 (NIV), the disciples gather around Jesus as He sat on the Mount of Olives. Jesus had previously departed from the grand temple. He opened a dialogue with them by saying "not one stone shall be left upon another," referring to the temple (Matthew 24:2 NIV). This was a prophesy about the destruction of the temple by the Romans in 70 A.D. Then the disciples asked Him three questions: When will these things be? What will be the sign of your coming? What will be the sign of the end of the age?

First, Jesus told them many will come in His name, saying they are the Christ. Don't be deceived. Over the centuries since then, many have come, and many have even said they were Christ. Sadly, many were deceived. Why? I believe they didn't read the Book and know the signs. If you are aware that there will be deceivers, you can be much more selective about who you will follow.

He also said there would be "wars and rumors of wars" (Matthew 24:6 NIV). That's kind of a constant occurrence. Somewhere in the world there is a war going on. But He admonished, don't be afraid, these things will happen, but the end is not yet. There will be famine and pestilences, earthquakes and persecutions, these are the beginning of sorrows. There will be false prophets and lawlessness, right will be wrong-and wrong will be right. Not yet! Does it sound to you, as it does to me, that all these things are happening now? Yes, they are.

Another benchmark we need to be aware of is the love of many will become cold because of the lawlessness. Often, within a person's heart, when our basic needs are met, we can be rational and make good decisions. However, when our basic needs are deprived, no food, water or shelter for an extended time, we begin to lose our focus. Our compass shifts, and we get into great trouble. In this recent pandemic, there was real opportunity for this to happen. It hasn't, but, during Hurricane Katrina when the local government could not keep up with the needs of the people, it began to get very unsafe, physically and emotionally. That is when a leader who claims to have the answer can step in and take over.

That is also where we as believers have the opportunity, and the responsibility, to share with those who are unaware of the signs to look for. Let's look again at Matthew 24:14 (NIV).

In my very humble opinion, this is the benchmark holding up Christ's return. In His love and compassion for us, He wants to see one more life redeemed, one more person He died for come to Him. He says clearly and in a very easy to understand instruction: the gospel shall be preached in all the world *then* shall the end come.

I don't know if you ever looked at the end time this way; we have a responsibility to usher it in. We have had it for over 2,000 years. We cannot grow weary of it, and we cannot give up on it. We do need to always have that goal before us and always keep our hearts engaged for God and focus on sharing Jesus with as many as we can.

Back to the question, is this the end? No one, not even Jesus knows when the end is. Only God the Father has that metric. I do know that He will not come until everyone has had the opportunity to hear. And I know it's closer today than it was yesterday!

Question: How many countries have not had a clear Gospel message presented to them? Look it up. That's where our evangelism focus should be.

plus ultra

"Look, he is coming with the clouds," and "every eye will see him, even those who pierced him"; and all peoples on earth "will mourn because of him." So shall it be! Amen.

Revelation 1:7 (NIV)

Years ago, my husband and I went on a tour of the Moravian Tile Works and Fonthill Castle in Doylestown, PA. It was an amazing tour of a lifetime of work by a very eccentric and very creative man, Henry Mercer. The home he lived in was virtually all concrete because he had a crippling fear of fire. He was amazingly creative in tile work, but only after he discovered he didn't have a talent in other forms of clay work such as vases and bowls. I would highly recommend going to see this National Historic Landmark. All 16,000 of the tiles on the floor in the Harrisburg, PA capitol rotunda were crafted by this very creative man. The history of Pennsylvania is told through those small squares and rectangles of glazed clay. As a creative person myself, I am in awe each time I view them.

One of the fascinating tiles I saw in Doylestown had a phrase in Latin carved into it. I saw this phrase repeated many times on many different tiles, and it intrigued me. What does it mean? Finally, I found more tiles with this phrase in the gift shop. I asked a clerk, "What does this mean: 'Plus Ultra'?" I didn't know if it was a local motto, a team motto, or even a political mantra. Remember this man was very eccentric! Well, when I found out what it meant, I was somewhat enraptured! The phrase, in Latin means, "more beyond."

My finite mind went on a vacation right then and there, "more beyond." It encapsulates every dream, every wish, every hope for our future in two words!

daily gems to spark your spirit

What do those words, "more beyond," bring to your mind? Right now, it may bring something you are planning in your near future. But remember, there is still something far beyond that. Look up at those clouds. Someday, in clouds just like those, we will see Him! Does your heart race hearing that? Re-read those words in Revelation 1:7 (NIV), "every eye will see him." I am just blown away! He is coming again; it's sooner today than yesterday, but we still don't know when.

In our day-to-day lives, with bills and a myriad of responsibilities, we can push His return to a corner in the back room. Yet, we don't want to be so engrossed in the responsibilities of this life that we don't hear the rumblings or the clear note of trumpet sound or don't see the signs of clouds parting and feet peeking through.

We must always be on high alert. For, in a moment when we are not paying attention, He may come!

Question: Will you be ready for His appearing? It is the most critical question you could ever ask yourself. Be honest. Your eternal destination depends on this one answer, and there is "Plus Ultra," more beyond!

sparkling!

In the same way, let your light shine before others, that they may see your good deeds and glorify your Father in heaven.

Matthew 5:16 (NIV)

Have you noticed how we are drawn to items that sparkle? I'm not sure how it happens but if we are watching something at a ball game, a picnic, even in church, as soon as someone moves a hand with a diamond, it catches the light and our attention! Girls, remember when you got your diamond engagement ring? When I came in the house with the ring on my finger, the family immediately saw the sparkle and crowded around me to get a better view.

Imaging if we as believers "sparkled" like that? Imagine walking into a room and a crowd gathering around you asking, "What is that sparkle I see?" That is what the scripture above is imploring us to do in Matthew 5:16 (NIV), "let your light shine." When I read that, I realized that it did not say, "tell everyone you sparkle." It did not say, "put an article in the newspaper listing when you sparkle." Nor did it say, "rent a billboard and post it on a busy highway for all to see your sparkle." It says, "let it shine for others to see" (Matthew 5:16, NIV).

Like the diamond that catches the eyes of those around you, when you do a good deed people around you will catch the sparkle, and they will ask: Who? What? When? Why? Where? How? Would you do such a thing?

Bang! Opportunity is knocking at your door. Open it and share the answers to those questions. Your Heavenly Father will be glorified.

Sparkle. Let's take the six questions journalists ask to get their story, and we will get our answers. First, who? Who should sparkle?

Well, just like the girl with new engagement ring, when Jesus changes our hearts, we *will* sparkle! We will not be able to keep ourselves from sparkling!

Second, what? What has made this change that is making us sparkle? It is the promise God gave us: I am with you, nothing to worry about. Sparkle season!

Third, when? As soon as possible, show your sparkle. No need to wait until you are in church or Bible study, you can sparkle everywhere! There are no laws against sparkling either, so sparkle away!

Fourth, why? Imagine for a minute you won the Publisher's Clearing House. You get the prize, plus $7,000 a week for life! Your head would spin; you would sparkle! You would sparkle for money. You spend it either foolishly or wisely. There is an end to the cash flow. But sadly, that sparkle will fade as people ask for money, and they don't get as much as they want. However, imagine you have just signed the deed for a property in heaven. The deed also says you will have everything you need, you will never be sick, you will never die, and you will be living in the same development as the Creator of the universe, God! I am sparkling just writing this!

Fifth, where should we sparkle? Everywhere we see darkness. People are sad, discouraged, hopeless, and weary. A sparkler in the crowd brings a little light to their faces and a spark in step. Just the knowledge that there is still hope and you are sharing it with them will bring a sparkle in their eyes and a spring in their step.

Sixth, how do we sparkle? This is the best one. We don't need to know how. I have seen many people either get up from an altar after giving their heart to Jesus, or after I have prayed the sinner's prayer with them, or even when I see them the next time after they received *sparkling!*

Jesus in their living room with a TV preacher. You just cannot help it. You will sparkle!

I don't know about you, but I think we need a lot more sparklers in our world. Do you know how we can get more? Share the light from our sparkler. The amazing thing is, we will lose nothing by giving away some of our sparkle, and they will gain eternity.

Go ahead, sparkle, and share it!

Question: Have you checked your sparkle recently? Does it still draw people to Jesus?

emerald—trusting

Bloom where God has re-planted you

He replied, "Every plant that my heavenly Father has not planted will be pulled up by the roots."

Matthew 15:13 (NIV)

When the season begins to cool down getting ready to go into autumn, I begin to think about my outdoor plants. I enjoy them all spring and summer as they go from that little plastic pod from the nursery to plant in containers on my deck. I visit them every day and water like crazy. Late in the summer, they are now large, lush, and beautifully arrayed in colors. Then, they go back downhill. But in 2020, I did some research on bringing plants indoors and overwintering. Great information about this process can be found online.

As with everything, there is a process. Now, I am not going to tire you with that process here, so don't shut the book, please. I just want to make the point that, yes, those beautiful plants you nurtured all summer can be brought indoors. They do require different care tips and will respond differently for next year, but with care, they will return!

Sometimes that is the case with us. We live in a place for a while, develop roots, get comfortable in ministries and a church, and establish friendships. Then life throws you a curve ball. A spouse passes away, a job is relocated, someone gets sick and you need to be the caregiver. Your comfortable and predictable world goes haywire. You are being re-potted.

Remember I told you that some plants can be successfully brought indoors? Some of us can successfully be relocated as well. It kind of takes a lot of the same steps.

Before moving the plant, or yourself, trim it down. The plant needs to be trimmed back to about one half of its lush self. When it comes to us, look around at what we really need. If you are like me, much of what we have in our homes can be given away, sold, or tossed so we can move without as much stuff to pack and unpack. This includes checking the plant for disease or insects. Well, if you are thinking you don't have those, think again! What if you examine yourself for any hidden bad habits? This is an opportunity to begin again without any of those old pests. Maybe your spiritual walk as had some "disease." Leave any doubts behind as you move forward to your new space.

I look around again at my little colorful garden. I am not looking forward to the work I will have to do to get these plants comfy in their new, indoor home. Yet for me, the knowledge that my beauties will be safe and warm inside when the howling blast of winter comes, makes the work a joy not a chore. The feeling of accomplishment as I check for disease, look for insects, trim them back, and finally bring them into a warm well-lit and loving environment is worth the effort. Just like this is a safe place, even a temporary one, for my plants as they look forward to next spring outdoors in their "real" home, we look forward to our heavenly home.

Re-potting, it certainly has its benefits. You might want to try these tips even if you are not moving. They are good for the soul, and you will flourish.

Question: Have you inspected your own self recently? If we want to flourish as believers that examination is necessary on a regular basis.

my Christmas wishlist

Not giving up meeting together, as some are in the habit of doing, but encouraging one another —and all the more as you see the Day approaching.

Hebrews 10:25 (NIV)

Our Christmas 2020 season was a little bit different than what we were used to! Many of us were not comfortable being around crowds, so we were not going to parties or gatherings. Many pageants and Christmas performances were cancelled or virtual. So many interactions with people came to a halt! Even some churches were back on a "virtual" schedule!

If we sat and thought for a minute, I believe we would realize that we need each other! We miss the interaction with other people during the course of each day. My husband and I had the opportunity to bless three widows in our area with a visit, a prayer, and a dinner. Our church provided the dinners, we just had to deliver them, with several other people delivering to many others.

Well, that was an adventure. The addresses on the list were very clear, and we had a GPS, but that did not prepare us for the actual site. The first woman's address said "R." We tried to get to the rear of the home, but the steps were a little wobbly! We made it, with my husband's help. Then there was a stairway up to a deck on the rear home. It was gated! I used to do surveys door-to-door. A gate meant "keep out." My husband came to the rescue again. He opened the gate, went up the steps, and knocked on the door! We met, for the first time, a lovely woman. Chatted, then prayed, and gave her dinner for Thanksgiving.

The next woman we could not find! Would you believe, as we were looking intently, she called us on the phone? God is so good; He knew we needed help! So, we found her, chatted a bit, prayed with her, and gave her a dinner.

Our last woman was so easy compared to the first two. GPS took us right there! A beautiful new apartment complex for seniors. We actually went into her home as she wanted us to see it. We chatted, prayed, and gave her a dinner. We left, and as we got into our car, she came running, slowly, out to our car. She wanted to give us a gift: banana bread! That was so sweet (pun intended) of her.

I was so thankful for this small adventure. Each of those women represented a former couple to me. I knew two of the husbands, each woman was eager to receive the chat, prayer, and dinner. Once again, I was reminded that we are all connected, and we all need connections.

"Lord, please show us where we can be the 'connection' someone needs right now so they can make it through another isolated day." Amen!

Though I didn't expect to receive anything from the ladies, after all we were ministering to them, it was a blessing to us to have received a gift showing appreciation. Our official Thanksgiving Day is gone, let's not forget that every day we have something to be thankful for. Let's express that always!

As I am getting ready for Christmas, I am making my Christmas wish list. I just want to be remembered! I want a chat, a prayer, and dinner is optional!

Question: How about you? What is your Christmas wish list?

f.a.i.t.h.

> For by the grace given me I say to every one of you: Do not think of yourself more highly than you ought, but rather think of yourself with sober judgment, in accordance with the faith God has distributed to each of you.
>
> Romans 12:3 (NIV)

On morning during my prayer time, I began to wonder why some people just readily accept what is told to them and some don't. Why do some people get so fearful about what is going on in our world and some see it as part of a bigger picture? I sometimes think people are like the six blind men who were asked to describe an elephant. The first man touched his trunk and announced the elephant is round like a snake. The second blind man touched the end of the elephant's tusk and said the elephant is like a sword. The next man said, no, the elephant is tall like a tree, after he felt the leg. A smooth wall is what the fourth man said after running his hand on the elephant's side. The fifth man felt the elephant's ear and announced it to be like a fan. The last man felt the tail and stated that the elephant is like a rope. An argument ensued as each man believed he was right. None were really wrong, but none were right. They did not have the complete picture of an elephant. We don't have the complete picture either.

When we only "look" at the world by what we can see in the natural, of course we are not getting the full picture. We live in an environment where God dwells and where He is always at work. When we view everything through the lens of Christ and the Word, everything just looks so much different and so much better.

When we look at the world in "accordance with the faith God has given us," we have the blindness the world places over the truth removed (Romans 12:3, NIV). We can see clearly with F.A.I.T.H: Facts Accepted In The Heart.

First, we need to look at the *facts*. But when the facts we hear are so confusing, misleading, and restrictive, who do we listen to? For truthful fact filled information, run to the Bible. But does the Bible talk about the things that make us fearful? Yes!

> I will say of the LORD, "He is my refuge and my fortress, my God, in whom I trust." Surely he will save you from the fowler's snare and from the deadly pestilence. He will cover you with his feathers, and under his wings you will find refuge; his faithfulness will be your shield and rampart.
>
> Psalm 91:2-4 (NIV)

When we read this verse, and others like it, we are encouraged, our faith is built up, and our fear is shot down.

Accepted. The word accepted indicates, to me, that there can be information we will not accept. When you hear the negative pronouncements come out of the mouths of media, politicians, billionaires, medical people, and so on, you do not have to take it in! You can listen Jesus to the experts but run it through the "filter" you know at truth from God's Word. If it does not align, toss it out. If it is truthful and helpful, absorb it into your behaviors. Listen, put it in a box in your head somewhere, but don't put it in your heart, the seat of emotions. We don't need that information telling us how to respond.

In The. Two little words connecting what you hear to where you store the information. When you get the information from the right source, you can place it safely "in the" right spot There it will overshadow and downplay the erroneous information you receive from the aforementioned sources.

Heart. Finally, your heart, the designated seat of the emotions. The heart can be fickle, it can be kind and gentle or rude, fearful or fruitful. Who is the master of our hearts? We are. We have the control button, the steering wheel, the switch to turn those emotions any way we desire. Only when we develop a maturity in life can we respond with the correct emotion. When a two-year-old has a temper tantrum, it is much more acceptable than when a thirty-year-old rants. Developing a maturity in Christ develops our emotions even further. With the Holy Spirit living in our heart, our world of emotion is different. They should be controlled, loving, and helpful. This takes a lot of training in the Bible and practice. It is a blessing.

F.A.I.T.H. We can allow the facts written in the Bible to penetrate our heart and make monumental differences in the way we perceive the world. We can find out truths and act on them, rather than accepting every new idea flying around. I encourage you to look at events through the eyes of faith. I believe you will be encouraged.

Question: Is there some news you have heard that has you especially distressed? Drop it at the doorstep of Jesus, He will handle it for you!

how are your casting skills?

Cast your burdens on the Lord, and He will sustain you; He will never let the righteous to be shaken.

Psalm 55:22 (NIV)

I watched as my young sons stood on the bank of a pond fishing. Not a care in the world. They knew somewhere nearby in an adult was watching over them. They had already been given all the instructions: "Don't get too close to the water," "Keep the life jacket on," "Watch where the pole is at all times," "Don't swing the pole around." If you have ever gone fishing with a little one for the first time it is a lot of instructions before beginning to have the fun of catching a fish. But just wait. I am pretty sure that's the way it is with every new adventure. If we want to learn how to do it right, we will listen. I remember sewing with my mom, painting with my dad, driving a car, reading a map, skiing, and the list goes on. First, you get the instructions.

Think about it. When we take a few minutes, or longer, to get the instructions before we begin, we are more likely to be successful and have fun. I know a kid who doesn't like to get the instructions. He thinks he knows how to do it before even trying. This kid seems to end up frustrated more often than not. He drops the entire project and walks away angry. You see, there is usually someone who has done what you plan to do before you did it. They know a little more than you, having had the experience already. When we glean the information they have, it helps us to make less mistakes. When we are too prideful and arrogant to listen, disaster awaits!

Now let's take a look at the verse again. I want to revisit it for a minute. Another version says, "He will take care of you" (Psalm 55:22, NLT). Knowing I was nearby and cared for them, helped these my boys have confidence while they were fishing. They know if they run into a problem fishing, someone who cares for them will help them. It must be like a security blanket wrapped around nice and tight. The first part of the verse, "cast your cares on Him," has a much greater impact knowing He cares for me (Psalm 55:22, NIV). When someone has our best at heart, it gives us a great assurance. We know God always has our best in His heart.

I am reminded of an ancient Jewish Rabbi who was carrying a heavy load as he walked. He passed an Arabian tradesman with a caravan. The Arabian said, "Take your burden and throw it on my camel." The Rabbi did so. What a relief the Rabbi felt! No heavy burden to weigh down his shoulders and give him pain.

We know there is One who has already carried the weight of our burdens on him. He will not grab them from us, no more than the Arab did to the Rabbi. He has made the offer, "Throw your burden on me. I will carry it for you!" Have we done that? Are we listening to Jesus as He makes this offer? Maybe we are like the kid who says, "I can do it myself," with pride and arrogance. How does that work out when we do it that way? We often stress, destress, and take it out on those around us. We don't cast our burden on the One with the answers, the knowledge, the experience, the strength. We need to work on casting skills!

Question: Are you still carrying a burden?

it's in there

And I will put my Spirit in you and move you to follow my decrees and be careful to keep my laws.

Ezekiel 36:27 (NIV)

Do you remember your first taste of cake? Did it taste like baking soda, or raw eggs, or a glass of cold milk? No. Yet all those ingredients are in cake and needed to make cake. No one had to tell you it was delicious and prompt you to eat it. The desire for cake was already in you. That indicates to me that there are certain attributes that are in our DNA. They don't have to be learned or prompted or encouraged. They come along in the package God made called you!

I am sure you have encountered this with children. We need to teach children many values and characteristics for them to become good people and citizens. We don't ever teach them to talk back, ask why, pinch their sibling, or leave their toys scattered everywhere. Somehow, they learn that on their own! That is also part of the package, the sinful one.

Think about your children for a minute. Your love for them, that overwhelming, lay-down-your-life love did not have to be taught to you. It grew in your DNA, and you could not resist it if you wanted to.

Father God has placed that type of love in each one of us! Think about it. At creation the spark that God energized each of us with, is *Him*! We are His children; therefore, just like we have that great inbred love for our children, a love that does not need to be taught to us, a love that we would risk or give our life, that, and greater, is the love God has for us! And yes, He did lay down His Son, in reality himself, so we could live with Him.

If you have any loved ones that are living outside the safety of salvation, today's verse is a great one to hold on to. That "spark" for God still lives inside them, it just needs to be ignited!

We have many plants in our home. I like a plant that brings green and filters the air at the same time. One of my plants, nicknamed "ZZ," stopped growing and started shriveling. I watered it, moved it, fertilized it, re-potted it, but nothing helped ZZ start growing again. I placed it in the garage planning to use the pot for something else in the future. We pretty much ignored it. About three months later, with no water, no sun, and no attention, I saw a green shoot. It kept growing and more popped out of the dirt. I took ZZ back into the house near a sunny window and gave it water. It is now a beautiful full green plant.

Inside that little ZZ plant was the power given by its creator to be re-born. That's what I'm talking about. Never give up on that "spark" God put into your loved one and in you. Continue to pray that the spark will get a jump start somewhere and their heart will not be able to resist Jesus!

Question: Do you remember a time when you needed a jump start for your faith? What was it that prompted you to move?

that's impossible!

And if the Spirit of him who raised Jesus from the dead is living in you, he who raised Christ from the dead will also give life to your mortal bodies because of his Spirit who lives in you.

Romans 8:11 (NIV)

It is impossible to comprehend in our finite minds just how the infinite mind of God works. That is why so much of our belief system must be accepted by faith. We just don't have the brain power to comprehend the mind of God, and we never will. Just like we wouldn't expect our kindergarten student to figure out higher math concepts or recite the alphabet in Greek, we can't expect that we will ever know how the mind of God works.

Think of this for a minute: The God of the universe, the one who set the galaxies in orbit, set the deposits of gold in the earth, established all people, colors and races from the three sons of Noah, is the same God who made the rules for how every minute particle and cell functions and duplicates. This same God cannot break the rules that He established. It's impossible for him to do. The concepts of "faith, trust, and belief" are difficult concepts for us to accept as human, prideful people; nonetheless, we must accept them. It's the only way. Crossing that bridge from death *in* sin to death *from* sin, accepting that Jesus took those sins to the cross, comes with the promise of eternal life with Him. When we believe that Jesus was raised from the dead, we can also believe He will make our own bodies alive to Him and His teachings. Where before belief, just like the disciple Thomas, we doubted, now we can believe. Some things must be believed to be seen!

Question: Have you experienced something that with the natural mind was impossible?

transformers: more than meets the eye

Do not conform to the pattern of this world, but be transformed by the renewing of your mind. Then you will be able to test and approve what God's will is-his good, pleasing and perfect will.

Romans 12:2 (NIV)

If you are a baby boomer, you probably remember seeing commercials for Transformers. My two boys always had them on their wish list for new toys! Transformers were pretty fascinating toys. Each part of the car could "transform" it into a mechanical hero.

When I taught second grade, I really enjoyed showing the children the "transformer" insect, the butterfly, and what it goes through each spring. I purchased a butterfly cage and set it up according to the directions. It was such a great learning experience as the children watched each part of the transformation process unfold until a painted lady butterfly finally emerged from the cocoon. As the egg transformed into a caterpillar, we were amazed. Then, the caterpillar transformed into the chrysalis, or pupa, and we were in awe. But when that butterfly inside the chrysalis began to shake, struggling to escape, we wanted to help! It wanted to get out. As the children watched the pupa shaking as it hung on the branch, the most assertive child always tried to open the cage and help. Each year, I had the same response. I had to stop them in their tracks and explain the process to them. You see, the little butterfly inside the cocoon is trying to flap his wings, giving them strength and drying them from the material in the cocoon. If that process is stopped by an overzealous observer, the butterfly can never regain the strength in its wings, and it dies. It can't fly, as a result, it can't find nourishment from flowers, and the beautiful creation God designed for our enjoyment is lost.

Well, the Bible implores us to become "transformers" ourselves! We have the capability of becoming either conformers or transformers. Let's explore this. I often listen to a group of women as they sit together and chat about the day. Well, one will say something like "Did you see the notice about our rent? It's going up again." The first lady says, "Yes, I saw that! Can you believe it? I am still recovering from the last rent raise." The second lady says, "I know what you mean! My rent payment takes up the largest percentage of my money. The third lady says, "And, they have not made any improvements around here." You get the picture. I guess its human nature to jump in on the proverbial band wagon when on person starts a bash fest. Let me ask you, does it do any good? Does it help the situation improve? If you answered "no" to both those questions, then you understand the value of being a "transformer."

In Apostle Paul's book to the Romans, he tells them, *do not* be conformed to this world (Romans 12:2, NIV). I am thinking one way we easily become conformed to this world is through our speech. When one person bashes the weather reporters, it then becomes acceptable for all of us to trash them. Same with doctors, lawyers, politicians, and on and on it goes. Without thinking, we want to agree with the person talking. What if someone in the group had the courage to have a different opinion? "Yes, I did see the notice about the rent increase. I am so thankful that this place covers all the utilities! They all went up this year, even more than my rent will go up." That would really throw that group into a tailspin. They were all ready to agree with the negative woman, now they have to stop and think! Now, they can become "transformers" with the woman who was thankful.

In our daily lives, we must be "transformers" in our thoughts. The Bible instructs us to do so: be transformed by the renewing of your mind (Romans 12:2, NIV). You are the only one who can direct your mind to a more positive and helpful thought process. Especially as we can see the end of the tunnel quickly approaching, we need to "transform" our mind to a mind that is open to the new changes, open to maybe some setbacks, open to being a helper instead of a hindrance to this process.

Be a transformer instead of a conformer. They are more than meets the eye!

Question: Are you a conformer with the crowd, even when you don't agree? Can you try a different approach and be a transformer and trend setter? I believe since God told us to be "transformers," that is what He would like us to be. When we become transformers, we reflect the positive attitude God always has! Let's reflect Him to the world.

what are you leaning on?

Trust in the Lord with all your heart and lean not on your own understanding; in all your ways submit to Him, and He will make your paths straight.

Proverbs 3:5-6 (NIV)

I am sure we all remember a time in a social awareness class when our teachers posed this experiment: Someone stands in front of a trusted friend and falls backward "trusting" the standing friend will catch them. Unfortunately, you cannot always trust that friend to catch! My husband knew of a teacher he worked with who posed that question to his middle school students. Everyone stood in place, but when the time came to "catch," the boy didn't! The boy in front fell, crashing to the floor and hurting his head. The boy who didn't catch thought it would be a funny prank and he would gain some status from his peers. But his plan backfired. Instead, they ridiculed him unmercifully until he threatened, then executed, a death wish-on himself! So incredibly sad. Our words and actions matter. They truly can bring life or death.

In today's scripture, we are instructed to physically place our trust in the Lord not in our own understanding of the situation. The implication is that before you act or react to any situation, lean on the Word! Every single situation we face in life has already been addressed in the Bible. Amazing, isn't it? Thousands of years ago God inspired over thirty writers to give us all we need to live life to the fullest in God's instruction book. We just need to read it!

So, before you "lean" on anything for too long, check out what the Bible says about it! When you place your trust in God, you never have to worry about falling. He will catch you every time!

daily gems to spark your spirit

Question: Can you recall a time when you chose to lean on the Word of God for an answer or situation in life?

what do we do now?

As you know, the Passover is two days away-and the son of man will be handed over to be crucified.

Matthew 26:2 (NIV)

Looking at the scriptures in Matthew 21 (NIV) after Palm Sunday, you might notice Jesus teaches much more about what type of character traits His believers should portray. He knew his time with them was drawing to a close and he still had so much to tell them. He still used parables, knowing the religious leaders were standing on the sidelines listening to every word.

He talks about having faith to move mountains as they would need that type of faith (Matthew 21:21, NIV). He shares about the fact that while all are invited to come to Him, few will be chosen (Matthew 22:1-14, NIV).

Still the Sadducees would listen to challenge and try to trip him in his words. Often, they ask ridiculous questions like this one: Who would a woman be married to in Heaven if she had been married to seven brothers and they each died? I can only imagine what Jesus is thinking as this is just a waste of the precious little time he has left on earth. He admonishes them again saying, "You are in error because you do not know the scriptures or power of God" (Matthew 22:29, NIV).

Finally, he asks them a question and stumps them.

While the Pharisees were gathered together, Jesus asked them, "What do you think about the Messiah? Whose son is he?" "The son of David," they replied. He said to them, "How is it then that David, speaking by the Spirit, calls him 'LORD? For he says,

'The LORD said to my LORD: "Sit at my right hand until I put your enemies under your feet."' If then David calls him 'LORD,' how can he be his son?"

Matthew 22: 41-45 (NIV)

After that answer they did not dare ask any more questions of Jesus.

He went on teaching about what was to come in the end times, continuing to implore them to be ready for them in more parables: parable of the ten virgins and the talents, the parable of the sheep and goats in Matthew 25 (NIV). He also encouraged them to help others in need in Matthew 25 (NIV).

Then, the religious leaders of that time had had enough. With their power over the people and their cash flow hanging in the balance, they assembled and hatched a devious plan to get rid of Jesus. The followers of Jesus were oblivious to how they were being manipulated. God was not! This was all included in His plan.

The feast of Passover was approaching. The chief priest, Caiaphas, wanted to kill Jesus but not during the feast because he was afraid of a riot. Funny thing, that's exactly what happened!

Each year, Passover begins at sunset. Passover reminds the Jews of God's faithfulness in "passing over" all the Jewish homes that painted the blood of a lamb on the door posts. Ten severe plagues hit every home that did not have the blood painted over the door. Passover reminds us as Christ followers that the blood Jesus shed on the cross was for us, it was our pass over.

Question: What does Passover mean to us today?

wings

> I said, "Oh, that I had the wings of a dove! I would fly away and be at rest."
>
> Psalm 55:6 (NIV)

"Look Mom, I can fly!" My son called me to the backyard as he practiced with his "super" cape and mask I made for him. As he jumped off the back deck (the equivalent of two steps), I cheered for him and my cape making skills! I thought about how fun it would be to fly! Any time the task gets difficult or the conversation gets too hot to handle, just reach for the mask and cape and escape.

Now, I remind you, God tells us with Him, nothing is impossible. Yet, in the reality of nature as He planned it, we can't fly. It's for the birds. We also can't live underwater without technical help. But it would be nice.

In this Psalm, David is seeking an escape. He wants to fly away or wander away, but he wants to get away. From what? His "friends." We often want to see our friends, especially when we can't. Not David! I think it has something to do with the kind of friends he had. He says,

> If an enemy were insulting me, I could endure it; if a foe were rising against me, I could hide. But it is you, a man like myself, my companion, my close friend, with whom I once enjoyed sweet fellowship at the house of God, as we walked about among the worshipers.
>
> Psalm 55:12-14 (NIV)

We have probably all had a friend we have had to part with over the years. Maybe a betrayal like David had, maybe just a change in your focus or lifestyle, or even a move in address. Whatever the reason, it still stings!

I have had all of the above circumstances for losing a close friend. When I became a believer and my habits, mouth, and preferences began aligning with those of Jesus, friends gradually slipped away. In many ways, it was a good thing. The temptation to follow them was no longer there. Still the sting of rejection took time to heal.

I believe in David's case the lure of being a friend of the king tarnished when the king did not give in to the friend requests. When we have some kind of influence, we can often get requests that we are happy to help with or find to be out of line. It is our choice to oblige or say no and risk losing a friend. My husband often says, "We deserve what we tolerate." It appears that David did not tolerate what did not align with God. Do we? For the sake of holding on to a friendship, do we overlook some things that bother our spiritual conscious?

When the Lord removes a friend from our lives, it is often for our benefit. Be the superhero you were meant to be. Don't stray from the flight pattern set out for you by the Lord. He will send another friend. Just be patient.

Question: When you have had a friend depart, looking back, can you see the benefit?

garnet—steadfast

do, or do not, there is no try.

All you need to say is simply 'Yes' or 'No'; anything beyond this comes from the evil one.

Matthew 5:37 (NIV)

Did you know that May 4th is "*Star Wars*" day? "May the 4th be with you." It's a play on words I was not familiar with until my grandchildren introduced me to the series. You see, back in the day when the series started in 1977, I had no interest in the series and didn't even have children yet! I was pretty sure I wouldn't like something that called people "masters." Only God is master! Over the years my understanding grew, as well as my love for my grandchildren and their interests. I began to see the series differently.

I began watching the series with the first episode, *The Phantom Menace*, although that is not the way they were introduced to the public. I fell in love! Why? Because through the presentation of each character and their growth, I saw how the influence of good and evil is so subtle but always there. Throughout the series, I watched as sweet Anakin was lured to the dark side with a promise that Palpatine would be able to bring people back to life after he had visions of his secret wife dying. When his beloved Padme died in childbirth, and he could not raise her from her deathbed, it was too late, he switched to the dark side and became the evil Darth Vader.

That is a simplistic overview to give you a look at how sin is portrayed. The enemy of our soul has no new tricks or tactics. Just like the enemy in *Star Wars* used deception, destruction, and death to lure Anakin into his trap, our enemy does the same thing with us today.

My favorite character in *Star Wars*, however, is Yoda. The old, funny-looking green character. He often talks a little backwards but makes sense anyway. He is the guy who took the scripture in Matthew 5:37 (NIV) and turned the words around but kept the meaning.

That is our focus for today. Yoda, the Master Jedi of around 900 years old, told Luke Skywalker, "Do. Or do not. There is no try." Many times today we have the "I'll try it" mentality, the "If it doesn't work, well, at least I tried" mentality. I believe that in our scripture today is this nugget of motivation, "just do it." We are so easy to bail out of something that, not long ago, we said, "the Lord told me to do it," or, "I prayed about it, and the Holy Spirit told me to marry him." Six months later you see the divorce announcement in the paper. We do not serve a schizophrenic God. He says about himself, "I change not." "Jesus Christ is the same yesterday and today and forever" (Hebrews 13:8, NIV).

He says, "If you said you were going to do it. Do it." No excuses, no ifs, no buts! When we don't do what we say, disaster strikes. Hearts are broken when promises are broken. Lives are lost when people abandon their responsibilities. Trust is just a hollow word when you cannot stay away from the thing that trips you up.

Please think first before you make a promise, sign on the dotted line, or tell someone "trust me." You are sealing your words with your honor. If you don't plan on keeping your word, what will the other person think of you? What will you think of you? What will God think of you?

The Star Wars series is considered a space opera. It is full of adventure, romance, betrayal, a bunch of kooky characters, and imaginative planets. Yet under all the drama, I hope you will find some hidden truth in Yoda's words. Let them be motivational to you. They have been to me.

do. or no not. there is no try

Question: If you are a fan of *Star Wars*, you have probably found some truths as well, maybe in the outer rim? If not, what are you waiting for?

do you want to be a model?

We are therefore Christ's ambassadors, as though God were making his appeal through us. We implore you on Christ's behalf: Be reconciled to God.

2 Corinthians 5:20 (NIV)

When I was a teenager, it was a very popular dream among the girls to become a model. When a group of girls got together, we would peruse fashion magazines. We would try to dress like the girls in the photos, do our hair the same way, even pose to see how we might look in a photo. Of course, it was only a dream. It was very rare in our area of the state that there would be any modeling opportunities, at least legitimate ones anyway. The concept of modeling just made us feel special, important, and noticed.

In reality we *are* models no matter where we are or what we are doing. It is a rare individual who has no one watching them at some point in their lives. Have you ever worn a new outfit and felt like every eye was on you? Have you ever tripped on a step and felt like everyone saw it? What you do or say right after you trip is what you are modeling. If your young children are with you, they are making a mental record of how you responded to that trip. You might even see your response repeated by them the next time they trip.

The scripture for today says we are Christ's ambassadors. When we have an ambassador in another country they are supposed to be "modeling" the behaviors and customs of the United States to that nation. When we have an ambassador from another country here, we can expect to become familiar with the customs and culture of their country as they "model" them for us.

When believers were first called "Christians" in the book of Acts, people in the city of Antioch were calling believers "little Christ." I am not sure they meant that as a compliment! Yet it stuck and was very accurate in its description.

We, as believers, are modeling Christ to the world in everything we do and speak. Think for a minute about the time you heard something from the mouth of someone you just didn't expect to hear. Maybe it wasn't foul or vulgar, just a little angry or judgmental. You probably made a mental note about them. When a person who believes you to be a "step above" in your Christian behavior then hears a nasty comment about someone else, well, you are modeling.

As models for Jesus, He is a designer that is head and shoulders above anyone else in this world. We need to always be aware that we are modeling behavior to the world by which they will be judging Jesus. When a runway model wears a famous designer's clothing line, it is a big responsibility to make them look perfect. When we are claiming to be Christian, it is a big responsibility to make Him look perfect because He is! We won't always get it right but if we are always aware, we are modeling behavior that exemplifies Him, I believe we will be more careful as we live for Him.

Question: How are you doing with modeling Jesus?

prayer: focus

Ask and it will be given to you; seek and you will find; knock and the door will be opened to you. For everyone who asks receives; the one who seeks finds; and to the one who knocks, the door will be opened. Which of you, if your son asks for bread, will give him a stone?

Matthew 7:7-12 (NIV)

So many verses in the Bible tell us to pray. And we really want to pray. Yet, there is so much in our lives to pray for it can be overwhelming. But we know we must pray. Prayer is really a conversation with God. How awesome is that when you think about it? We, God's creation, have the opportunity to carry on a conversation with *the* Creator of, well, everything! It is often difficult though because we don't get responses immediately, so it feels like a monologue.

I have been using a prayer metric I would like to share with you today. With it, I can spend a little more time on one element because I am not praying for everything every day. I hope it helps us all have a prayer focus. It is fairly easy to remember. And every element we need to pray for has a "focus day," so all through the day you can be thinking of and praying for one thing and be focused in prayer.

Of course, there are our "regular" daily prayers and our "emergency" prayer requests. Those do not fall into this metric. But for the "general" elements we should be praying for, this may help.

So, I use my hand as a reminder for our first five days. My thumb is closest to me, so my thumb represents those closest to me. You can start this on any day, but I suggest Monday.

Monday will have you praying for family, relatives, cousins, friends, close associates, and anyone else you want to cover in prayer. Call them out by name or write them out if you wish. The more modalities you use, the more focused it will be. This tends to bring these people to my mind through the day, and I can shoot up a quick prayer right then. You may not know what is going on in their lives that they need that prayer to cover. Or you may get a call from someone you are praying for right then. This happens with my sons and mom sometimes.

Tuesday is your pointer finger. This will remind us of those who "point" the right way for us to go. Pastors, teachers, leaders, maybe bosses. Give special attention here to calling them all by name. Often as I say a name, another one I had not thought of pops up. I do write them down so the next week, they get prayed for again.

Wednesday, our "tallest," middle finger reminds us of the government officials. I heard that groan! Hey, if believers don't pray for them, nobody is praying for them. Especially in election years, pray for wisdom for them all. You can get names of your own senators, representatives, and legislators online. It is important to pray for them by name and even the issues as well.

Thursday is our ring finger. This is actually our weakest finger. Thursday's finger reminds us of the weakest in our society that desperately need our prayers. Pre-born babies, children, the mentally or physically disabled, and our large elderly population. You may also add the homeless and incarcerated in this group. This may be another forgotten group.

Friday, our pinky reminds us of the people we can take for granted until we need them. Our police, firefighters, ambulance workers, and sanitation workers are just expected to be there when we call them. Also, mail and package carriers to ensure we can be provided with what we need. Other workers we depend on are restaurant workers and road workers, but the list is endless!

Saturday has no finger to remind us, but if you ever get sick, this is the group you want: medical professionals! From the nurse's aide to the surgeon, we need these people to be on their game every day. Your prayers can help. List your doctors and nurses by name. Don't forget your pharmacist, therapist, and any technicians who administer tests. All these people need patience dealing with the sick daily. They also need wisdom to do it correctly!

Sunday, the Lord's day. What better time could there be to pray for people who need the Lord! It may be family, friends, or someone the Lord put on your heart. It might not even be someone you know now. It may be someone you saw in church that morning. Remember, this is our responsibility to bring in the lost and subsequently hasten the Lord's return. This is our job: bring them in. And it starts with a prayer to soften their heart.

I hope this metric for prayer covering is helpful to you. I find it frees me up to spend more time on each daily segment of our population, and I believe my prayers are more specific and effective. It also has given me some very heartwarming moments while thinking of specific people who mean a lot to me rather than just a very general prayer for everyone who is sick today. Think about the fact that if this caught on with other prayer warriors, a lot of prayer would go up on certain days for certain groups. The Lord says our prayers are a sweet aroma to Him. Something like that might be just what could change an outcome of a situation for the better. Your prayer helps. I say, "Prayer changes me!"

Question: Can you remember when prayer changed the outcome of your situation?

it's the truth, ruth

But Ruth replied, "Don't urge me to leave you or to turn back from you. Where you go I will go, and where you stay I will stay. Your people will be my people and your God my God. Where you die I will die, and there I will be buried. May the LORD deal with me, be it ever so severely, if even death separates you and me." When Naomi realized that Ruth was determined to go with her, she stopped urging her.

Ruth 1:16-18 (NIV)

Ever look up at the night sky? On a really clear night you can get a great exposure to many stars, the moon, and even some "unidentified by the naked eye" masses of, well, stuff. I remember looking at something shiny with a smoke trail coming from one end and lights on the other end. No, wait, that was an airplane. As it got into my range, I saw "Southwest" written on the side! For that type of study of the sky, I really needed a telescope.

I feel like for a more in-depth study of the Word, we also need a telescope. Oh, not the kind needed to study stars, but the kind that looks deeply into the past of the people and their stories, then describes how they all fit into God's timeline.

For this study, I would like to introduce you to Ruth. I'm sure you are somewhat familiar with Ruth's story. She was a Moabite woman who married an Israelite man, Elimelech. Now, this was at a time when Judges ruled in Israel. They may have been good, fair Godly judges, but they were often evil. At this particular time there was a famine in Israel, so the family of Naomi and Elimelech left the area of Judah and moved to Moab where there was food, but the people were not Godly. The couple had two sons, but sadness found them when, first, Naomi's husband, then her two sons died in Moab. Since Naomi and her family were living in the land that her daughters-in-law, Ruth and Orpah, came from, she told them to return to their own families. Custom was that if one son died, the next son in line would marry the widow. There were no more children for the two women to marry, so Naomi implored them to go home and be taken care of by her father once again. Ruth would not have it! She was committed to Naomi and wanted to stay with her. Naomi planned to return to Judah and her relatives rather than stay in Moab, an ungodly country.

Let's pull back for a minute with that telescope, shall we? Looking at a larger picture, Ruth had lived with, cooked with, even worshipped with Naomi during her courtship and marriage to Naomi's son. I believe she saw something different than what her life was like at home and she wanted it!

Back to the story. Naomi and Ruth return to Judah. A small town, it was made clear to everyone that Naomi was back, and she brought her daughter-in-law, the Moabite with her.

After all the return greetings and settling in took place, Naomi had a job for Ruth. Since they were both widows with no one to support them, they could "glean" grain from other fields. Since the reapers could not capture every grain that fell, they left some behind so people like Ruth, and other poor people could at least get some food to sustain themselves.

So, let's look through that long lens again. Ruth goes into the field of a man named Boaz. She could have gone to any field because they all were all supposed to allow "gleaners" but she went to Boaz. Do you remember Rahab? She was the woman that hid Joshua and Caleb under the straw on the rooftop, keeping them safe from the warriors in Jericho. Rahab was a redeemed Gentile, prostitute, and the mother of Boaz! Are you seeing how this telescope is catching connections further and further beyond our present events? So, sweet Ruth goes to glean at the field of Boaz. He immediately recognizes her as someone he has not seen before but someone he wants to know a little better. He blesses her with extra food and an offer that she can return to his field all the time and she will receive special treatment by his workers. She must have been a cutie!

When Ruth gushes all this information to her mother-in-law, and Naomi realizes the magnitude of the blessing her daughter in law received that day, she begins to think. She alone knew that Boaz was related to Naomi. Ruth was not even from that country, maybe she didn't even have the same 'gleaning' custom in Moab. Maybe she did not have the "kinsman redeemer custom either!" But Naomi knew! She gave Ruth explicit instructions to get and keep the attention of Boaz. It worked. Now Boaz responded by telling Ruth he will redeem her, but there is a closer relative than himself he must check with. Once all the formalities were done, Boaz was free to marry Ruth and redeem her. They married, and now looking ahead in our telescope, this Moabite woman became the mother of Obed. Obed is the father of Jesse. Jesse is the father of David. David became the King of Israel. Fourteen generations later, Jesus the Messiah was born through this line of ancestors!

So, through the ancestral line of a gentile prostitute, and a Moabite widow, Jesus, the perfect Lamb of God, enters this imperfect world. It is fascinating to me that our God who has all resources at His fingertips, could have planned that Jesus be from a long ancestry of Kings, prophets and priests. Instead, He chose a prostitute and an idol worshipper. Through our "telescope" we clearly see in the story about Ruth and Boaz, the "foreshadowing" of *the* Redeemer coming to carry our sins to the cross. I don't know about you, but with His ancestry, I have no problem feeling that I fit in to the family! I'm pretty sure that's the way He planned it.

Question: What do you think about God using these types of people in the ancestry of His perfect Son?

king of the mountain

> Now to the King eternal, immortal, invisible, the only God, be honor and glory for ever and ever. Amen.
>
> 1 Timothy 1:17 (NIV)

I remember when I was a kid, a long time ago, we played "king of the mountain." Part of my neighborhood was an old, unused coal mine. So, this leftover stuff called "culm" just piled up until it made a good-sized heap, about six-feet-tall. For those unfamiliar with "coal country," a culm dump was the small shards, powder and coal left behind when coal was extrapolated from the mine.

Several kids in the neighborhood would climb the mountain and claim to be "king of the mountain" until a stronger or wiser kid came up from behind and knocked the king down. It wasn't a parent-approved game because, sometimes, someone got knocked down and often got hurt! It was a rough game, and we were often covered in soot and dirt from the culm, as well as small slashes from sharp shards.

Even when we read in history about kings and monarchs, climbing to the top and forcing someone off seemed to be how they operated. The monarch with the strongest troops, the wisest planners, and the most money became "king of the mountain" or country.

That's just not how it is with our God! He is King of the universe. He doesn't have to fight anyone for it, or even just claim it like we tried to do. He just *is*! In fact, when asked who He was, that is what He said: "I AM" (Exodus 3:14, NIV). That was all He needed to say! "God said to Moses, 'I am who I am. This is what you are to say to the Israelites: "I am has sent me to you"'" (Exodus 3:14, NIV). This means that anything we need, God is! Because He is:

The One and Only wise God.

The Creator of the Universe.

The Rule maker.

He knows our past, present and future.

He loves us just the way we are.

He has the answer to our every question.

He will forgive our sins and heal our diseases.

He gives us peace that is beyond our comprehension, even in difficulties.

He leads and guides.

He promises to never leave us or forsake us.

This list could go on and on, but just these ten items give us a great start on who God is and what He has done and continues to do.

Question: How many more attributes of God can you find? Which ones mean the most to you?

my rock obsession

Tremble, earth, at the presence of the Lord, at the presence of the God of Jacob, who turned the rock into a pool, the hard rock into springs of water.

Psalm 114:7-8 (NIV)

I like rocks! I know it may sound odd, but just the permanence of rock intrigues me! I have often painted them and used them around my garden or to decorate areas in the summer. I have even sold them, and I have painted rocks with requests for certain artwork. And, I admit, I have made a few "pet" rocks with my grandchildren just for fun. I even have a rock from Israel that a friend smuggled in her luggage when she went there. I will never paint that one.

While painting them, I examine their shapes, textures, and surface structures. Each and every one of them is different. I have never held, carried, or pushed a rock to another place that remotely resembles another rock. As rocks are distinguishable from other rocks, it makes sense that every person is different. Yet, God tells us that not two of us are alike, even though we were personally created by God. Even identical twins don't share the same fingerprints. You are unique, one of a kind. There is no one else like you! As we think on that for a minute, we should expect that each of us has a different relationship with God and a different "call." We each have a personal relationship with God, yet we expect that all Christians should behave the same way. We know that God created each of us as individuals, and we have a benchmark that believers have to meet to be bone fide believers.

What do I mean? Well, we often think that our children should become like cookie-cutter children. We send them to school where they often wear uniforms. They have snack and lunch all at the same time often when they aren't hungry. They play outside all together and are expected to keep at the same pace of study as the rest of the class. I do understand that it would be very difficult to treat a class of children as individuals. We just do not have the ability God has to have individual relationships with each child in a classroom setting. I do wonder, though, if we did have a more personalized, more geared toward our strengths, type of teaching maybe we would be getting more out of school.

So many times, in the Bible, we read references to rock. The Old Testament states that we were cut from the rock: "Listen to me, you who pursue righteousness and who seek the Lord. Look to the rock from which you were cut, and to the quarry from which you were hewn" (Isaiah 51:1, NIV). Rock was used as an engraving medium: "And they were inscribed with an iron tool on lead, or engraved on a rock forever" (Job 19:24, NIV). There are many instances where the Lord is referred to as our rock: "The Lord lives! Praise be to my Rock! Exulted be my God, the Rock, my Savior!" (2 Samuel 22:47, NIV). "For who is God besides the Lord? And who is the Rock except our God?" (Psalm 18:31, NIV).

I think my rock obsession is very valid. The rock is a tangible thing that I can hold and be reminded that I stand on the Rock for my salvation! I have rocks around my house, in my plants, outside around my patio. I am never far away from thinking about my Lord. I hope you look at rocks from an entirely new prospective.

Question: What reminds you that you stand on Jesus for your salvation?

sacrifice

> Therefore, I urge you, brothers and sisters, in view of God's mercy, to offer your bodies as a living sacrifice, holy and pleasing to God-this is your true and proper worship.
>
> Romans 12:1 (NIV)

Sacrifice. Now that is a word we don't like very much in our "I've got to have it all" mentality. It implies lack, hardship, less than, and doing without. But Paul sends a letter to the Romans saying, "offer your body as a living sacrifice" (Romans 12:1, NIV).

What could Paul be trying to say here? Well first off, God initiated the sacrifice. Remember the Hebrew people were expected to bring animals for sacrifice. The animal was taken from the person and killed on an altar to give thanks to God or offered as penance for sin.

In the Hebrew language, "sacrifice" comes from the root word "korav" to "come close to." Let's unpack that thought for a minute. God instituted the sacrifice of the first fruit, the best. And He wanted the blood or life from the animal. The sacrifice was an offering for a sin or a thanksgiving to God. Now, track with me here. If the root word for sacrifice means "come close to," I believe God is telling us that a way to draw close to Him is to sacrifice. He showed us what that meant to Him when He sacrificed His son to draw close to us. God's son was the living sacrifice that allowed us to get close to God. Maybe you have always looked at it that way, maybe not. Let's go back and look at Paul's statement again.

Paul implores *us* to become "living sacrifices." First off, that is a relief! God doesn't want us to do anything that would compromise our physical bodies. He just won't ask that. Some "religions" do expect you to do crazy things that might get you killed or in trouble with the law. Not our God. The "living sacrifice" He does expect from us is to stay away from sin! Sinful lives will tear us away from a Godly and productive life.

Still, Paul expresses the words of God saying this is "true and proper worship" (Romans 12:1, NIV). When we offer our bodies, mind, and spirit to Him, we keep ourselves pure and holy and are worshiping God in pure form. This is not a Sunday morning in church kind of worship. It's not a blast the worship playlist and sing along worship. It's not even the reading your Bible kind of worship. It is live every day in everything you say, read, do, even eat and drink to please God. It is reasonable for Him to expect it; He gave us His son!

A butterfly, mouse, bear, bird, any other animal, everything that grows, all of earth and space have been programmed by God to behave in a way that is unique to them. When they live out their lives behaving in the way they were created, they are "living sacrifices." So are we! When we find out who we are and what God expects us to do, then when we do it, we become the "living sacrifice;" we become pleasing to God. We are giving Him true and proper worship!

The advantage for us is when we are living our lives within this "worship zone," we are the happiest and most fulfilled. Let's take our cue from creation and do what we were created to do!

Question: Have you found out what God wants from you for His "living sacrifice?"

seek his face

If my people, who are called by my name, will humble themselves and pray and seek my face and turn from their wicked ways, then I will hear from heaven, and I will forgive their sin and will heal their land.

2 Chronicles 7:14 (NIV)

We need to recognize God is in control, and we are not. Today, we look at "pray, and seek [God's] face" (2 Chronicles 7:14, NIV). We know that prayer is just communication with God. Though if you think about it, communication with the God of the universe is not a "just" anything. It's huge! When we communicate with someone, we usually expect an answer. I say usually because there are people who just like to dominate a conversation. They tell you all the minuscule details of their lives. In fact, sometimes the things they tell you have no relevance to the story, but oftentimes you cannot interject a thing. Those people may do that when talking to God too!

They give a point-by-point retelling of their day, then a list of their needs, then they are off before God even gets the opportunity to respond. Here's the thing: He will always respond when we seek His face. The face is where all our emotions are shown. On our face, our mouth can respond also. Seeking God's face takes time.

Have you ever held an infant and given them a bottle? It takes time. You may be in a hurry, you may try to rush it, but there are very messy consequences. Same here. When we don't allow God to respond to our requests, we may end up in a mess! God will never steer us in the wrong direction. We, however, may do that all by ourselves if we are not listening.

I would encourage you to take the time to actually sit in God's presence. Start off by thanking Him for everything you have in your life including health, strength, provision, family, friends, church, a job. I could go on and on, but you get the picture. God is so generous with us. We cannot begin to thank Him enough, but we can try. Then, tell Him just how amazing and magnificent He is! Remember, He's the Creator of the entire universe, time, people, and every good thing. Somewhere in your prayer, stop and listen. That's when I hear the still small voice of God. He may just show me a smile, He may give an answer to something I asked or just make a comment. But you know in your "knower" that it was God! It takes time.

We only have so much time allotted to each of us. Don't waste it, spend it with God almighty!

Question: Would you like to hear what God is saying to you? Or are you fearful of what He might be saying?

someone's watching you!

The LORD watches over you- the LORD is your shade at your right hand.

Psalm 121:5 (NIV)

At the shore in Ocean City, Maryland, I opened all the curtains on the windows completely because I like the view of the ocean. However, on one side of the room the window faced the adjacent building of condominiums. I was fascinated by the number of rooms in this building and the fact that, from my vantage point, each balcony looked like the door to a small cubby in a storage system.

Each morning, I made my coffee and went to the table by the windows. I opened all the drapes wide and the windows if I could. After taking in the magnificent ocean, my interest turned to that "wall of cubbies" next door. Every morning, it was a different scene. Sometimes all I saw out there was the colorful towels and swimsuits of the vacationers behind the doors. Sometimes, I saw a man come out and smoke a cigarette or a couple watch the ocean together. Other times, it was several children still in their pajamas as they looked out and dreamed about their day. Once, I saw four people come out of the lowest rooms. Their balcony was on the roof. They got out, walked across the roof and just watched the majesty of the ocean. I chuckled thinking that none of these people knew I was watching them. I did not know them, and they were watching me too! I was in my robe!

Up until that moment, it never dawned on me that they could see me. Then, I made the leap: we are always being watched by someone. You know what I mean. Recently my husband and I were at my mom's apartment building. She had given us the code to get in, so we used that instead of calling her. Immediately, the manager ran out of her office and explained sternly why we shouldn't have the code and why she now had to change the code for the entire apartment building. She was not a happy camper. There was a right way to get the door opened. We were being watched. While you are at the grocery store alone with your list, talking to yourself and comparing prices, someone is watching. While you are at a football game and your team doesn't get the points, someone is watching. What did you say? Who heard you?

With that thought in the back, or front, of your mind, how will it change your behavior? Maybe you don't really care who is watching. Maybe you care a great deal. We should care. Not only are there people all around us who can watch how we behave and judge our merit, but our Heavenly Father is always watching. Remember the childhood song "Oh be careful little...what you..." and you fill in with each of your senses? Yes, it is childish, but it's true! I like to think that our Heavenly Father is so loving that He watches us to find something good He can boast about just like He did with Job. But I am afraid that is not always the case since the Bible tells us "all have sinned and fall short of the glory of God" (Romans 3:23, NIV).

If we can get this phrase imbedded into our hearts, I believe we would be better behaved as people in general and believers specifically.

Question: Have you ever been a people watcher? Did you realize someone is watching you?

the triplets

And now, dear children, continue in Him so that when He appears, we may be confident and unashamed before Him at His coming.

1 John 2:28 (NIV)

I have some questions for you. How long has it been since you thought of yourself as a child? If you have grown children, do you still think of them as children? Remember the way you felt when your parents caught you doing something you were told not to do? Or do you remember the look on your children's faces when you caught them doing something they weren't supposed to do?

Now, let's talk about the fact that in God's eyes, we are still children! Today's scripture specifically calls us children. In our eyes when we reach ages eighteen to twenty-one, we are making most decisions on our own. We may have our own apartment and be out from under Mom and Dad's roof and rules. We may have jobs, a car, a spouse, or even our own children. But still, God is calling us "dear children" in His Word (1 John 2:28, NIV).

Let's look at what a child is. I was just at someone's home with five-month-old triplets. Imagine that. This single mom had to run some errands, get groceries, prescriptions, formula, and diapers. So, in our church, we have a group of people who have signed up for three-hour shifts while she does the necessary things that keep a household running. And since my hubby and I are retired, we volunteered!

Of course, we first got a quick overview of their three different schedules. Each baby had their own bottle and formula. Their cribs had each of their names. That was helpful, but only if you knew who was who! Sara needed medication within thirty minutes after eating.

However, she fell right to sleep after her bottle. Ben guzzled his bottle. We changed his diaper, and he went back to sleep. But Kira, well, she was not having any of it! Her shock of red hair and her cry told me she was her own little person, and she was just not wanting that bottle! She was usually breast fed and didn't want a bottle just because her mom was not there. It wasn't Kira's fault.

Obviously, we felt bad but rocking, walking, cajoling, music, and even my singing just didn't help! When Mom came to the door, she knew just what the problem was. We left quickly, knowing we had done our job. Now, she and she alone had to do hers.

Yes, we are still children too. Some of us are like Sara and Ben. We follow the rules, go by the book, do as we are told. We are compliant. Some of us, like Kira, want what we want, and we want it now!

Think about being Ben and Sara as you stand before God. "Lord, I did as You asked me to do. I followed Your plan to the best of my ability, with Your help. I was confident You were always there to guide me and help me when I needed it. I can stand here with a clear conscience." And Kira? Well, she represents those of us who like to push the envelope. She makes her own schedule and rules and forgets where her life and everything she has come from. She will also stand before God one day, the Creator of the universe, and I fear she will be ashamed. She didn't do the simple little things, like drink her nourishment, and live it.

How many of us are like Kira? We think we know better and push God away, the only One with the hope, the answers, and the help for our lives. These three precious babies will grow, change, and make decisions to follow the Godly path or not. One thing that will not change, they will always be God's children.

Who do you identify with? If you still behave like Kira and you are an adult, take a minute and re-evaluate your life. Are you listening to your Father God or yourself? Kira, Ben, and Sara are still infants. They will grow and change, learning new patterns and ways to achieve their goals. However, they will always be children of God, as are we. We will always be connected to Him with "heart strings." Some may try to break those strings, but it's impossible. We will always be attached to our Creator.

I don't know about you, but in my home, things always went better for me if I did the right thing the right way the first time. I find it's the same with God. If we live by His book, our lives will be better and we can stand before our Father, unashamed.

Additional Reading: Romans 8:16-17 (NIV).

Question: As a child of God, can you remember a time He asked you to do something and you disobeyed? Have you asked for His forgiveness?

opal—kindness

april hope

> The next day John saw Jesus coming toward him, and said, "Behold! The Lamb of God who takes away the sin of the world!"
>
> John 1:29 (NIV)

When I began writing these devotions in March 2020, I had no idea we would be in the throes of a global pandemic. How could I have known? I did, however, know the One who did know. I find it so amazing that He would orchestrate this miniscule piece of the universe so it aligned with this stressful time so many people could be comforted with hope. When I wrote March "comes in like a lion," I thought I was talking about the weather, not the coronavirus.

Then in April 2020, most of the United States began a lockdown to continue until the end of the month. But April comes in like a lamb! A lamb that is pure, no guile, sinless, and just a comfort to look at and spend time with. The hope of April. The Hope of Jesus! John the Baptist, the forerunner for Jesus, announced, "behold the Lamb of God who takes away the sins of the world" (John 1:29, NIV). Our hope is in Him!

I recently read about Ruth in the Bible. Naomi, Ruth's mother-in-law, wanted to change her name from Naomi to Mara because of the bitterness and sadness in her life. Maybe if we just change the name of this month to "April Hope," it will remind us God knows the end, and it's coming soon. In April, seeds and flowers begin to sprout, birds noisily fly everywhere, neighbors walk with their children and dogs. Hope.

Jesus said it best, "I am the resurrection and the life. He who believes in me, though he were dead, shall live" (John 11:25, NIV).

That is the Hope we have in Jesus: a forever life with Jesus in Heaven.

Though we often felt that our lives were over because the virus stole so much from us all, we also knew that God had the final word in the situation. What the enemy meant to use to steal our health, kill our bodies, destroy our livelihoods, God used to draw us back to Him. "What good will it be for someone to gain the whole world, yet forfeit their soul?" (Matthew 16:26, NIV). Our God was not the initiator of the evil virus. God only does good; it's His nature. However, He will take what our enemy meant to harm us and turn it around for our good.

Let's think. During the global pandemic, children were home playing with their parents. They were being taught by their parents. Husbands and wives spent more time together. People shared with those in need. They were looking out for one another. Churches figured out ways to connect on online. People questioned their own faith and looked for answers.

In Matthew 4:19 (NIV), Jesus told us to go fishing for men. This may be a time when the "fish" jump right into our boats!

Question: If you got sick enough to face death, would you know where you would go after death?

be an overcomer!

Do not be overcome by evil, but overcome evil with good.

Romans 12:21 (NIV)

Sometimes it takes an open mind and some information to turn an evil desire or action or emotion into a good one.

When I was just a young girl, every hot and sunny summer day, I went to the pool with my friend. It was a free local community pool across the street from my house. We called it "the oxie." There was a main street with a lot of traffic between "the oxie" and my house, but we were allowed to go there all summer. It was great fun, hanging out with friends, sunbathing on our towels, then cooling off in the pool. So, every day my friend Patty and I would put on our suits, grab a towel and a dime for an ice pop, and go.

One summer day while we were at the pool, I hid my dime under my towel for safe keeping while we went into the water. We had a grand time swimming, splashing, giggling, and diving for nothing in particular. When we were tired and wanted our ice pops, we returned to our towels, but my dime was not under my towel. It was nowhere to be found! Patty searched under her towel. We looked around the area in case it somehow rolled but nothing. I was devastated. I had never been a victim of a crime before, and I was indignant! Patty and I walked home sulking. No ice pops for us today.

Well, my mom was at home. When we told her the entire sad story, complete with dramatic enhancements, she answered, "Let this be a lesson for you, not all people can be trusted. You will just have to believe that the person who stole your dime must have needed it more than you did."

I went up to my room, and Patty went home. I thought long and hard about what Mom said. Now, dimes didn't come to us kids easy. We were not flush with money; however, the thought of a kid who needed my little dime made me feel sorry for that child. I don't know if I said a prayer for them, but I do remember feeling better about losing my dime. In fact, I often think of that story when I see those in need. It motivates me to do good and give, so they don't have to do evil and steal!

Many years later, someone stole my purse out of my car. It was of much greater value than my dime. My license, checkbook, and even Social Security card were in it. In the days that followed the theft, I searched near the crime scene for any traces. My store discount cards were tossed on the side of the road, but that was all I found. Another day passed, and the local police called me. My Social Security card was found by someone, and they left it at the police station. The next week my license was returned to me in the mail. I thought about this evil thing that someone did to me. I thought about the kindness of others, going out of their way to "overcome" the evil with good. I thought about my mother's words: "They must have needed it more than you." This time, I said a prayer for the person who took what did not belong to them. I prayed that they would understand that their action was wrong. But if they needed the money that badly for sustenance, I prayed that the Lord would bless them so they didn't have to steal. It was a comfort to me; the sting of the stolen items was gone and didn't possess my thoughts any longer. It did remind me that a thought through reaction can overcome an evil action.

Question: How about you? How can you be an "overcomer of evil" in your corner of the world?

divine appointment?

> But Samuel replied: "Does the LORD delight in burnt offerings and sacrifices as much as in obeying the LORD? To obey is better than sacrifice, and to heed is better than the fat of rams."
>
> 1 Samuel 15:22 (NIV)

My husband had a medical test done recently. Since they needed to put him under anesthesia, I had to go with him to drive him home. This was the first time I had experienced the new coronavirus safety protocols. We arrived at the facility and were greeted by a small table outside the locked entrance. A sign said, "Knock on the door and someone will come." My husband knocked, and a nurse in mask and plastic gown came out and sat at the table. She asked him a few questions, took his temperature, had him sign paperwork, and asked me for my cell phone number. Then she explained to me that due to COVID-19, I was not allowed to wait for him inside the building. I had to wait in the parking lot in the back of the building. I would be called when my husband was ready to come out.

I was a little taken aback. Since my husband was sedated, I wanted to hear what the doctor said about the test. My husband might miss something. But that was the way it was. I drove around the back and waited. It was a beautiful day, so I popped the trunk and sat in the hatchback to catch some rays. There was another car in the lot with someone in it waiting, but that was it.

Not too much later, another car pulled in in the space two spaces away. A very animated woman got out of the car and began putting bags from the front into the back. She opened her trunk and began muttering things like "where is it," "I can't find it," "I must have lost it in the move." Of course, I had no idea what she was talking about, but

I did say hi. She said, "I have lost my Social Security card." My heart sank! I had a wallet stollen once, and my Social Security card was in it. I felt her pain. All the horrors of what could happen if that card got into the wrong hands ran through my mind in a flash!

I tried to encourage her to slowly look through each of her bags. She said she did. She did it again. No success. Finally, I asked if I could pray for her. She said, "Please do." At the proper distance, I reached my hand toward her and prayed, loudly. We were in a noisy outdoor area after all. I asked our great God to open her eyes to be able to see where that card was and open her mind to the Holy Spirit as He revealed to her where she should look. I quoted, "Call to me and I will answer you and tell you great and unsearchable things you do not know" (Jeremiah 33:3, NIV). She thanked me and said she must be going to the Social Security office before the line grew to a mile long. We exchanged our first names, and she was off.

I continued to pray for Marlene. Then I got busy with some phone calls and such. Pretty soon, I heard my name being called. I did expect my husband to come out soon, so I thought the nurse was calling me from the door that he was ready. Nope, it was Marlene. She pulled up next to my car and talked so fast I could hardly understand her. It appears that on her way to the Social Security office a thought came to her. *Look in the black case.* She told herself, "You have looked in that several times already." When she arrived at the office, she reached down on the front seat, opened the black case, and voila! The Social Security card she had been searching for was there.

Of course, she thanked me profusely for the prayer. I reminded her it was the Holy Spirit who earned the credit; I was just the pipeline that God could work through. She was ecstatic. I told her I appreciated the fact that she came back to tell me. She explained that she had to! She said, "The Lord put you in my path to pray for me, I had to come back to thank you." When she left, I began to wonder how many times do we pray for a situation when the Holy Spirit prompts us, but we never know the result of our prayer? Then I thought about how many times we neglect to pray because we fear being rejected. We may have been the pipeline God wanted to use for an answer to a prayer. The next time fear stops you from doing something you believe the Lord is prompting you to do, think about Marlene. Would she have found that card in time without the prayer?

I found myself grinning and thanking Jesus for a real-life illustration of the Holy Spirit at work. Right in the back parking lot of a medical facility during a pandemic. Go figure!

Question: Have you ever had one of these experiences? I know I am not the only one. How did it make you feel to be used as "God's pipeline" for a blessing?

do you have a gift for me?

We have different gifts, according to the grace given to each of us. If your gift is prophesying, then prophesy in accordance with your faith; if it is serving, then serve; if it is teaching, then teach; if it is to encourage, then give encouragement; if it is giving, then give generously; if it is to lead, do it diligently; if it is to show mercy, do it cheerfully.

Romans 12:6-8 (NIV)

I like getting gifts! How about you? I like giving gifts too! When my grandson was younger, we loved to give him gifts. He was so comical when he would very slowly open it, then when he saw it, he would announce, "Oh, it's exactly what I wanted!" No matter what it was.

Our great, loving heavenly Father gave us the greatest gift: Jesus our Lord and Savior! But He loves giving us gifts, as most parents do, and he offers to give us a bunch more.

When and why do we get these gifts? No special occasion, just because He loves us so. It's funny to think about it but He has His "gift list" already made out. Not who He gives what to, like I do at the end of summer getting ready for Christmas shopping. No, His list is a list of awesome spiritual gifts He wants to give. He just has to decide who gets what gift! How does He decide? I cannot be absolutely sure, but I think He gives them when we ask for them. That has been my experience.

Let's look at that list of gifts He is ready to give. There are seven listed here in Romans 12 (NIV). Look them over and see if there are any the Lord has already given to you.

Prophesy: This is probably the most confusing and misunderstood gift. In the days before the written word, prophets were used to share information God wanted the people to know. These days, the purpose is different. First, let me tell you, it's *not* foretelling the future! It's a way to make known the will and way of God as it aligns with scripture. It's not scary, dark, or condemning. It *is* enlightening and encouraging. You can find more in Acts 2 (NIV).

Serve: This one is pretty self-explanatory. You will know who has this gift in your church because they are the "worker bees." Any time cleaning, painting, cooking, selling, or anything else needs to be done, the person with this gift volunteers. But it doesn't stop there. In the community or at their job, they are still serving. My friend who has this gift is cleaning up the table after a meeting while I am still chatting! This is not my gift, but it was Martha's in Luke 10 (NIV).

Encourage: This is an awesome gift when you are on the receiving end. I have been there. When someone sincerely gives you encouragement when you are hard at work with something, it spurs you to keep going. Barnabas was encouraging in Acts 11 (NIV). Motivating!

Teach: This gift goes far beyond the Bible study teacher or the pastor who preaches like a teacher. This is a gift that is used every day by the person who has it. I do have this gift, and I can say that from teaching grandchildren to women's group to how to make a bedroll for the homeless, I am in a teaching mode. This gift permeates every part of your speech and thought process. It is embedded in your personality. That may be the way it is for all the gifts; I am just not aware how it works for them. Hey, let me know, okay? By the way, Jesus is the master teacher and the best example for all of us who have this spiritual gift.

Give: All of us give when we are prompted by a story, a letter, a photo or another disaster of some sort. Our heart and emotion kicks in, and we give. But the gift of giving is a little different; it's on steroids! Giving comes so naturally to the giver that sometimes the family has to intervene so that the person has enough for themself! They would literally give you the shirt of their back. The widow showed her giving gift in Mark 10 (NIV). It's a gift.

Lead: When given the task of leading a group, there are the naturals. They know how to organize, plan, direct, and encourage to get the job done. Nehemiah was a leader. You can read his strategy for re-building in Nehemiah 1-5 (NIV). It is enlightening! If you have this gift, people will know it and gravitate to you when a job needs to get done. This one comes with great responsibility and criticism, so if you ask for this one you must be tough!

Mercy: This can also be a tough one! This is the one who shows compassion when others are walking away. Recently we have seen many people with the gift of mercy extend themselves to COVID-19 patients. After helping them in the worst times, if they don't recover, it can be devastating for the one who gives mercy. This is also the one who helps the homeless, the addicted, the depressed. This is the Samaritan who wrapped the man's wounds in Luke 10 (NIV).

You can probably see where your gifting is, or the gift you would like to have. We can ask God to give us a specific gift. Now, if you have a gift you are not using, well, you really should not ask for another one. But use the gift(s) the Lord gave you to bring glory to Him. Thank Him for the gifts, regularly. Exercise the gift and it will increase-just like exercising muscles. Also, neglecting the gift will cause it to atrophy. It will still be there. God doesn't take a gift away from you; it will just lie dormant.

Question: now that you are familiar with the gifts, what one(s) do you have? What one(s) would you like?

ezer

Surely God is my help; the LORD is the one who sustains me.

Psalm 54:4 (NIV)

I hope I caught your attention with that word "ezer." In Hebrew the word "ezer" means "a help." Many minor people in the Bible also had the name Ezer, a helper. We often name our children with a meaning that will go with them through their lives. This is a great name to have, in that respect.

In our days, however, ezer is much more than a name; it's a lifestyle. If you have a friend who exhibits this ezer attribute, keep them! When you have a need that a human can fulfill, you call on your ezer. I remember at the beginning of 2020, I had a cough and low-grade fever. This was when we were still able to get out of the house, but there was chatter of a bad virus coming our way. I had a plan to meet a friend for coffee, but I didn't feel well enough to go. She immediately texted me, "I'll make you some chicken soup!"

Just a couple hours later, she dropped off a bowl of homemade, Jamaican chicken soup and several honey and ginger tea sachets. I felt better just looking at this sweet gift she made for me! She was my ezer in my time of need. By the way, it was just a cold, gone in record time thanks to Karen's loving kindness!

When I think of today's verse, I think of that kind of help. He is the right-now-remedy to your particular need. Right now, in our area, there is a population of people that are mostly forgotten. They really need us to become their ezer! It's our homeless population. If you are thinking that it would never happen to you, think again. It sometimes only takes a family a couple bad blows and they begin a

daily gems to spark your spirit

downward spiral into poverty. If you have never experienced it, God blessed you to bless someone else!

I have a friend in Clarks Green, Pennsylvania. She knows someone in the Dominican Republic with great needs. In reality, it's an entire community in crisis. Just a bag of rice is life sustaining for them! Even some school-aged children in the United States would be without meals if they weren't provided in school! I just find that so disturbing in the United States: hungry children. So, what can we do to be an ezer? A lot!

I have listed a few non-profits in a previous devotion that do a fabulous job meeting needs. Maybe you have time and can help somewhere. Just a couple hours a week at a homeless shelter in your area is a very worthwhile way to spend time. There are many opportunities to help there. Of course, they also accept donations. My mom, husband, and I made and sold masks to raise money for our local homeless shelter. The shelter used the money to take in about twenty-five people at a local field house. That is a help to them and us! They are on the front lines too. Did you hear anything about them in the news?

I believe we can forget there is a homeless population in our areas. Everyone we know is housed and fed. My husband and I watched a movie that depicted a homeless woman's struggle. The star was Lucille Ball! It was the only serious role she ever did, and she was seventy-four years old when she did it. The movie is *Stone Pillow*. I recommend it highly.

She does a great job showing us what really happens on the streets after dark, when we get all snuggly, cozy in our homes with our snack and favorite program. They are fighting rats for a piece of garbage to eat, looking for a secluded cold staircase to sleep on, and still have to guard all their earthly belongs from thieves.

After volunteering at our shelter for a couple years, I can tell you, though it will take some time for the people to warm up to you, once they do, it's a very rewarding experience to get to be an ezer to someone often trying to come out of their pit!

Sometimes I look at all that the Lord has blessed me with. Most of us are very blessed in this country. Then I remember my friends on the street. Jesus said, "Truly I tell you, whatever you did not do for one of the least of these, you did not do for me" (Matthew 25:45, NIV). What can you give? Can you be someone's ezer today?

Question: If you were in need, what would you want someone to do for you?

gimmie that! i want it!

Keep your lives free from the love of money and be content with what you have, because God has said, "Never will I leave you; never will I forsake you."

Hebrews 13:5 (NIV)

The Christmas of 1960 something, all my aunts, uncles, and cousins were in our living room. My brother and I were showing the family our gifts: my new ironing board and iron, Steve's new Tonka truck and tool set, my new Tiny Tears Doll, but I couldn't find it. That was my favorite gift from Santa, and I lost it? Out of the corner of my eye I saw my cousin with my doll! I asked nicely, "Please give my doll." She said "No, it's mine." I yelled, "No it's not! I just got that doll from Santa! It's my favorite." I was starting to get upset. She refused to turn it over. I told her again in a very serious, high-pitched voice. I was older and bigger than she was. I was getting my doll back! I lunged toward her, leaping over gifts, wrapping paper, the dog, and a couple smaller cousins. She panicked and tossed it behind the couch. I started to cry. Her parents took her by the arm into the other room for a chat. My mom pulled the doll out from behind the couch. Her beautiful porcelain face was cracked!

Looking back at it now, I still feel the sting of that moment, and I still have that doll, crack and all. I realized my normally sweet, little cousin became a "bear of a kid" when her "covetous" spirit rose up in her. Did she get Christmas gifts? Yes. She had no need to go stealing mine, but that jealous monster rose up in her, and she reacted badly.

I think we have all had those moments. Now, we have not all reacted in that way, but we may have wanted to! Look at the verse above. It is great instruction about our conduct. Yet, if we are confronted with a situation then start looking for how we should respond in a Godly way, it's not going to happen. If we read, reflect, and even memorize this verse and others now, at a time when there is no provocation, it will be on file in our magnificent memory when we need it.

We, even as adults, have moments when we haven't been in control of our emotions. I have said this before: "Our body will never go where our mind has never been." Thinking about the correct, moral, Godly way to respond to life's unexpected situations is a big help to us when it does happen. How do we know what's going to happen? We don't, but He does. By reading the Word each day and meditating on it, or I prefer to "marinate" in it, the wisdom seeps into our pores. When something happens, and it will, the right response will have soaked in and now is there to be able to respond in a correct, moral, and Godly way.

Question: What have you been marinating in? Will it give you the response you desire to handle adverse situations?

God is more than enough!

If my people, who are called by my name, will humble themselves and pray and seek my face and turn from their wicked ways, then I will hear from heaven, and I will forgive their sin and will heal their land.

2 Chronicles 7:14 (NIV)

Life was a little confusing in 2020. Sure, washing our hands and giving elbow bumps was fairly easy. Even carrying hand sanitizer and disinfecting wipes everywhere was not much of a hardship. But my husband went to the grocery store one morning, and I didn't understand what was taking so long as he went when the store first opened and usually no one was there yet. Not so that day! He said the place was mobbed. Signs on things said, "LIMIT 2." There was absolutely no toilet paper! And many items were on pallets. The workers stocking couldn't get the items onto the shelves as people were taking them right off the pallets.

He came home in some kind of a confused dither. He didn't know what to make of it. Since it was senior citizens discount day, they were there in busses! They just stood staring like they were looking at King Kong. He felt very bad for their confusion.

My friend in Florida found the same circumstance in her local grocer. She only needed milk and toilet paper! There was *no* toilet paper and very little milk. She got one gallon, then thought she should get another, just in case. There are only two adults in her house. How much milk can you drink? Well, she thought better of it and only got one. *A family may need it and not have because I took an extra.* She thought as we all should be thinking! I called my son. He lives near Philadelphia, Pennsylvania. He sounded distressed and exhausted. He said he was going to work but using sanitary precautions. He felt confused.

I said before, "God has given us every answer we need if we look into His Word." The coronavirus crisis was no exception.

I can see the solution to this problem hanging as if in a cloud over us. It will stay hovered there until we take the bull by the horns. Until we muster up the troops. Until we humble ourselves!

Do you remember at the Tower of Babel? God confused the languages because people became arrogant and thought they could build a tower to reach Heaven? God had a different plan. Do you think maybe He looked down and saw how arrogant and disobedient we as a world had become? Did He see we put sports ahead of Him on Sundays, and so our sports were gone? Did He look at the amount of money we spend on cruises, trips, alcohol, even restaurants yet we forget the local homeless shelter or the children who do not have clean water in Africa?

May I suggest that we take this time, after so many of our activities have been curtailed, to re-evaluate what we are doing with our lives. See, we only have this one life, so if something happens, we are with God. If nothing happens, God is with us. He is the only One that matters, and He knows what He is doing!

Question: With the time God has given you, are you tithing it each day? With the money He allows you, do you tithe on that? How about your talents? Have you tithed on using your talent for God's Kingdom? The pandemic may just be a test run for future events. So, what did you learn and what are you learning?

handprints everywhere!

Give, and it will be given to you. A good measure, pressed down, shaken together and running over, will be poured into your lap. For with the measure you use, it will be measured to you.

Luke 6:38 (NIV)

"Go wash your hands good with soap!" I told my grandson, again. He touches everything and has no thought about what he touched before or what he will touch after. I stopped to think about that for a minute. We know that children are not the only ones who touch everything. We, as adults, do enough touching ourselves, our phones, remotes, knobs, faucets, money, and the list goes on. Usually, we are leaving fingerprints on furniture, doorknobs, dishes, books, phones, and so much more. There is no escape from the number of places we leave a trace of our DNA and our identity!

Think about this. If we have our identity in Christ, isn't it time we leave our "heart prints" with some of our DNA on others? I am sure your heart has been touched if someone sent you a "thinking of you" note. I know mine has. Or maybe you've received an encouraging text, even an emoji. Maybe an unexpected check came to your mailbox at just the right time with a note, "thought you might need this."

I would like to propose that we leave our identity in Christ on other people with a heart print! How? Think about how you feel when you get a phone call or text from someone? Do you know someone with small children or an elderly person who would appreciate a meal left at their door? Can you be a financial help to someone waiting for unemployment to kick in? Ask the Holy Spirit how you may be able to ease the anxiety of someone in your sphere of influence. Send someone a heart print of God's love.

I don't say this to instruct you without having done many of these myself. So, here is what I know from the doing: you will ease your own anxiety when you reach out to others. How so? Our Lord gave us the instruction, and His words do not fail. He said, in His Word, that the measure we use to give, will be the measure used to give back. I have realized we can't out give God. No matter how large our measuring cup is, He uses a bigger one to give back His blessings to us! Can we make it a priority during these last days to reach out in a way that will be encouraging for all? After all, when we do something for others it is what makes our Heavenly Father happy. When He is happy, there is no end to His blessings!

Question: Has the Holy Spirit been telling you to do something for someone? Have you done it? What's holding you back? Just do it! It may motivate someone else and they will pass it on.

compound blessings

Praise the LORD, my soul; all my inmost being, praise his holy name. Praise the LORD, my soul, and forget not all his benefits—who forgives all your sins and heals all your diseases, who redeems your life from the pit and crowns you with love and compassion, who satisfies your desires with good things so that your youth is renewed like the eagle's.

Psalm 103

I remember an illustration my math teacher did in front of the class in high school. He said you could take a penny and put it in a jar. Each day you put in double the amount that you put in the day before. At the end of one month, after doubling the amount you put in the jar each day, you would have one million dollars saved! We were all amazed. This was an illustration for "compound interest." I spent the evening doing addition problems to check it out. Of course, he was correct, teachers like lawyers know the answers before they ask a question. One huge disadvantage I found is at about the middle of the month you actually have to start putting in thousands of dollars. I knew it couldn't be that easy!

However, I believe we can use the same principle with blessings! Let me explain. Since God is always in the giving business, He delights when we give to others, without grumbling. When He sees us giving, He "compounds" the interest on our giving and gives it back to us. Now, we feel more charitable when we receive a blessing, and we give a little more. Well, don't you know, before long it comes right back to us again!

My husband and I have used this principle over and over. It never fails! I watched it recently with my mom. I wrote about how she is sewing for children in the Dominican Republic. She lives on a fixed income, so she is careful with her money. When we suggested that she drink a high protein shake daily to boost her nutrition, she was concerned about the price. Well, one of the residents in her apartment building received two cases of the drink, and she won't drink them. She asked my mom if she wanted them. My mom got them free! A returned blessing. She, in turn, is giving some coats that are too big for her to a homeless shelter. Someone else in her building offered her a bunch of clothes that don't fit her anymore. Blessing returned. You see how this goes right? I like to call it "compound blessings." You can try, but you just cannot out give God. But it is fun to try!

Of course, these are small examples of "compound blessings," but He does it on larger scales as well. When my husband and I were faced with an unexpected financial challenge years ago, we still continued to tithe, and give-cheerfully. We gave $100.00 to a group that came to the church. The next week we received…wait for it $1,000 from someone in the church who was nudged by God to give us the money. Funny thing, he received the money unexpectedly after he had given extra! We were the beneficiaries of that one, and it supplied our immediate need! A word of caution, we give because we are told to not with the desire to receive more, and God knows our hearts. Sometimes we are just blessed with health, peace and contentment. That's a "compound blessing" also.

Now, I do not advise that you give so you can get. But I would like to challenge you to try this principle. We are told to "Give, and it will be given to you. A good measure, pressed down, shaken together and running over, will be poured into your lap. For with the measure you use, it will be measured to you" (Luke 6:38, NIV).

Question: What kind of measure do you use when you give?

mission: focus

> I have brought you glory on earth by finishing the work you gave me to do.
>
> John 17:4 (NIV)

    I am speaking for myself now when I say that I have been in a rut! Not the day-to-night pajama rut but a rut, nonetheless. I think I'm kind of a homebody, and since that's what we were forced to do for much of 2020, I got very comfortable in my routine. Oh, I had a list, followed it for the most part, did work around the house, spent extra time in prayer, studied, kept in touch with people. Now, I am facing a different type of stress: return to business! Yes, I am stressed about it. Running here, teaching there, company, shopping, visiting, trips.

    So, the Lord knows all about us, right? He planned my Bible reading in Luke 10:38 (NIV). I am sure you are familiar with it, the story of Mary and Martha. Almost immediately I saw it! I have read this story so many times, even cite it in Bible studies, but this was a different thought. This was a light bulb thought!

    So, I believe each of us has been given a destiny by God. We have gifts and talents we can use to further His Kingdom. One of mine is writing. Over many years, I dabbled in writing. Yet, I never really knew what I was supposed to be doing for God with my writing, until recently. Why? Well, that's the focus of this post. When the Lord gives you a talent, He expects you to use it for Him!

    Here's the light bulb moment. I was distracted from writing for many years. Either I was busy with children or had to have a paid position or just didn't know what venue to use. Like Martha, I allowed so many of the distractions of this world keep me project-focused instead of mission-focused. Too often my gift was gathering dust in the corner! What's the difference? I mentioned my list up above. Now a list is a great incentive, but it should reflect our mission. Instead, I had my chores listed, the places to go, the people to call. I was obsessed with getting the list done before I did the mission-focused items. My day would be gone and side-tracked by project-focused item. Mission-focus would be gone, again. That makes someone happy, but not Father God.

My boss at a bookstore was a writer. I asked how she writes so many books. I think she had five in her series. She told me the Lord will not allow her to move on with her day until she writes. It did not have to be a whole novel or even a chapter. She just had to write! I call that mission-focused.

In the story of Mary and Martha, that was Mary. Her mission was to soak up every word she could while she had the living Word in her home. I would imagine just sitting in the same room with the Son of God would be a sublime experience.

I believe the Lord is holding back on His return until more people come to Him. I believe our mission-focus should be to invite them to come. We just invite; the Holy Spirit does the preparing of their heart, and Jesus forgives them. We just need to invite.

We each need to find out how we are best equipped to invite. Not everyone does it the same way because the people we invite wouldn't receive it the same way.

So, that's what the Lord told me this morning. For me, writing is the way I am reaching. Guess what? He wants to tell you too. Just ask Him what the best way for you is, with your unique set of gifts and talents, to reach others for Him.

We can't all be missionaries, but we can all be fishers of men and women! So, I have decided I will not put my writing on the back burner. When some busy tries to pull me away, I will stand firm and use an old slogan, "just say no." We don't have to be and do everything for everyone, we serve only one Master!

In the verse above from John 14:7 (NIV), Jesus reminds us even *He* was given a task to complete for His Father. Through His finished work, He brought God's glory to the earth. Our task is a bit different: we bring glory to the Father. We won't all do it the same way. Our talents are each different, but it must be our mission. We must be focused on it especially as the day grows nearer.

"Remember tells us to ask Him for information we have no other way of knowing. He will tell you the answer," (Jeremiah 33:3, NIV).

Question: What has God gifted you with that you can use to reveal Christ to others?

we light up the world!

You are the light of the world. A town built on a hill cannot be hidden. Neither do people light a lamp and put it under a bowl. Instead they put it on its stand, and it gives light to everyone in the house. In the same way, let your light shine before others, that they may see your good deeds and glorify your Father in heaven.

Matthew 5:14-16 (NIV)

Ever hear of the butterfly effect? It is a theory that a butterfly can beat its wings in one corner of the globe, and the weather changes halfway around the world with that one action of the butterfly. I'm not sure I believe that completely, but I do believe our very small actions can have a huge impact on the lives of others.

Let's break down what the verse above says: *you* are the light of the world. Go on. How can that be? *We* light up the world? Wow, that seems like a huge responsibility. It is! It means that you should always be on your game, always at your best, always projecting His light to the world. It doesn't mean we can't be real. When we hurt, we show it, but we still behave with the hope of Christ in our demeanor.

Let's think about little fireflies. They have a big job to do. That light is for their own protection. That little light keeps their predators away. Wait, what? Yep, that little light keeps predators from coming close and gobbling them up. It hit me like a light bulb turning on: we are the light of the world. Our light keeps the enemy of our soul away from us! Light dispels darkness and evil is dispersed. Fireflies' bioluminescence is the product inside them that keeps their light burning brightly, from their birth. We have Jesus in us. He keeps us healthy and our light bright. The bioluminescence has been used in many medical procedures and medicines. The light inside the firefly has healing properties.

Though that little firefly does not bite us, or really annoy us in any way, it really speaks loudly and clearly. I am here! The light inside me draws others to me, and it repels those that may harm me. The light I have inside me is beneficial for all mankind.

When I was praying about the title of my blog, mydailyfirefly.com, the Lord showed me the amazing power of that one little light to bring hope to your path. I pray that you can always be like a firefly, drawing others to you, and repelling evil from you.

Question: Do you believe you are the light of the world, lighting the way on someone's path? Giving hope in dark situations? Or has your light grown dull? Is it under a bushel? It's not too late to get it out and let it shine!

Thank you, Lord, for making such an amazing little creature to speak truth into our hearts.

pearl—heroes

eighty-five and alive!

With long life I will satisfy him and show him my salvation.

Psalm 91:16 (NIV)

My mom was smiling while holding eight-month-old Emmett, a friend's baby, on our deck. She turned eighty-five-years-old on June 7, 2020. Please don't think wrongly about my title, it's just that so many miracles have occurred in her life that *Eighty-Five and Alive* is also a miracle! Let me explain.

My mom was the fourteenth child in an immigrant family. Living on a shoestring and often government assistance, only ten of the fourteen children survived. Now, she alone is left from her siblings. My grandfather and grandmother migrated from Austria-Hungary before Lenin moved in on the country. I never knew my grandfather to ask, but I believe he could see "the handwriting on the wall." Bad days were ahead for Eastern Europe, as history would prove.

There was no emphasis on education for my mom, and she quit school in the tenth grade and began working in a blouse factory. That was when we had factories here in the U.S., and you could make good money if you were fast and accurate. She was!

After a few years, she met and married my dad. They moved to Bridgeport, Connecticut for better jobs. Dad worked at Sikorsky Aircraft; Mom worked in a factory. At that time, early 1950s, factories were everywhere, made everything, and jobs were plentiful. A couple years later, she found out she was pregnant with me. Life was good! When I was born, I was the first Martin grandchild. I was spoiled! But enough about me, my mom was amazing. She sewed beautiful clothes for me and kept me "spit-spot" as much as she could. I liked to get dirty!

Soon, my adorable brother, Steve, came along. My dad would say he had a "million-dollar family." We were a happy bunch, but my Russian Baba in Scranton, Pennsylvania was struggling to live alone after her husband died and last child got married and left the family home. My mom said it was time to go back and help her.

The stress of everyday life and a lower paying job took a toll on my Dad. He began drinking, until one day when I was about twelve, he was in a terrible car accident. He had many injuries, including severe brain damage. Two years later, at the age of thirty-five, my mom became a widow with two children to raise alone.

After three years, she married a man she met through relatives. Lloyd was a good man and took good care of my mom. He and his three children moved in with us. With no counseling for blended families, we had to navigate those waters on our own. Sometimes we swam; sometimes we sank!

One day in a very bad winter, roads were treacherous, and my mom experienced what we now know was a subarachnoid hemorrhage. She was rushed to the hospital. We were told she had a fifty-fifty chance to survive the night. She later had a stroke that left her one side weak. Two months later she returned home, eventually returned to work, and virtually all of her abilities returned. Of course, this came after much prayer for her and much praise to God for His goodness!

Not too many years later she experienced a heart problem. A valve was replaced, she recovered completely. She was complaining about her leg repeatedly. After she saw the doctor, we thought would handle this problem. The doctor said, "This is not a leg problem, Donna. It's a heart issue. No blood is going to that leg." A cardiologist confirmed it and performed triple-A bypass surgery on my mom. The doctor said this is the most difficult surgery that can be done. Praise God she recovered 100%, another miracle.

eighty-five and alive!

One time, she was prepped for a minor hernia repair operation. The doctor quickly returned after seemingly just taking her in for surgery. My stepdad and I thought, *Oh, no something went wrong.* We were wrong! God apparently healed the hernia, and no surgery was needed. Hallelujah!

Years later my stepdad developed Parkinson's Disease then dementia. My mom cared for him until he passed. She was widowed, again.

She is a conqueror of many other issues I have not even talked about. She quit smoking and drinking, she raised a grandchild, she went through children divorcing, she grieved the death of a daughter-in-law and the death of her oldest stepdaughter, and the list goes on.

So, you can see why I claim *Eighty-Five and Alive* for my mom. She looked brain damage, heart failure, brain hemorrhage, kidney problem, stroke, cigarette addiction, widowhood, and said, "By God's Grace, I will live and not die."

Mom, this is my tribute to you in this your eighty-fifth year. I pray for God's continual blessings and care. I love you with all my heart and pray I can face life with the same faith.

Question: Is there someone you know who has defeated all odds against them? Say a prayer for them and their example to you.

dad and donna marie

Fathers, do not exasperate your children; instead, bring them up in the training and instruction of the Lord.

> Ephesians 6:4 (NIV)

I was named after my dad, Donald. My dad grew up in Northeast Pennsylvania and moved to Connecticut for jobs. He did return when my mom needed to care for her mom in Scranton, Pennsylvania. He got a job as a fork-lift operator for Cocoa-Cola. We always had coke syrup in the house to use as an elixir when we were sick. It tasted good, though I'm not sure it worked.

My earliest memories of my dad were in Connecticut. He was a smoker. When we went to the petting zoo one time, a goat came up to him when he knelt to pet it. The goat ate his cigarette! I was amazed. That little goat just chomped away on that tobacco and paper! My dad was an awesome wood worker and made many items for me as a child. A step stool with a horse head on the ends, a small chair for my small frame, a rocking horse for my enjoyment. All were passed to the next generation and are gone. His greatest work out of wood was a sixteen-foot motorboat. He named it and hand lettered the sides: "Donna Marie."

When the circumstances of life brought them back to Pennsylvania, life got hard. My dad began to drink too much. When I was fourteen, he was in a severe car accident. He was never the same and died two years later. I still miss my dad. He was a fun and talented guy. I had plans to learn more from him.

I think of the fact that he was supposed to teach me to drive. He was supposed to be there to be the role model for my perfect husband.

He was supposed to be proud of me at high school graduation, walk me down the aisle at my wedding, hold my sons in his arms. He was supposed to be there for all the milestones that families enjoy together, but my dad was ripped right out of the photo!

I don't want this to sound like a depressing devotional, though it is maybe for me, I want the dads who read this to know something critical! *You* are important in your child's upbringing, and wellbeing. Only *you* can fill the shoes that will get your child on the right path in life. Please be there.

My dad had a smoking addiction that may have affected his health in later years and shortened his life. It was the drinking addiction that did him in, though, at age forty-one. Both of these habits, as well as many other habits we acquire over the years to "self-medicate" when life gets rough, have the potential of ripping you out of your child's picture of your family.

My granddaughter graduated from high school this year. She took photos with her parents that will always be in her heart. I was so happy to see that. I remember when my husband and I stood with each of our sons for this proud moment. These are foundational moments in your child's life.

So dads, please be careful, please take care of yourselves. Remember your prince and princess need their king dad, no matter how old they get. Please do everything in your power to be sure you stay in the picture. You are loved!

Question: what is your favorite story about your dad?

give me liberty or give me...

Stand fast therefore in liberty by which Christ has made us free, and do not be entangled again with a yoke of bondage.

Galatians 5:1 (NKJV)

By March 23, 1775, the American colonies had been forced to endure taxation without representation, searches and seizures without probable cause, the confiscation of firearms, and on and on. This had been going on for over ten years. The tyranny of the British Empire was unreasonable, and the Americans had had enough. Though they tried to remain loyal and reconcile their differences, they finally were compelled to break away in revolt. This was the forerunner for the American Revolution.

The drafters of the Declaration of Independence had a detailed list of the legal offenses they had against England. They saw these as much more than a list of isolated wrongs, but they saw it as a predetermined attempt to take away their religious liberties and reestablish the Church of England. We can understand Patrick Henry's words as he faced a return to the enslaving religion, after experiencing the liberty of the Christian faith, in whatever style he chose.

We now seem to be facing tyranny again. While our Constitution still says we have "freedom of religion." It still says we have a "right to bear arms." It still says, "all men are created equal." You may not recognize those attributes in our country today!

What is our responsibility? What did our founders do? It appears that they were able to only take it for so long. After trying all the ways, they had available to them back then, with no success, the brilliant document *The Declaration of Independence* was birthed. This was more than a mere written dream, it was a prayed over, fasted for literary piece of genius, guided by the Holy Spirit of God!

As the Revolutionary War was becoming evident, one of the drafters, Thomas Paine stated, "These are the times that try men's souls." We appear to be in the same condition. While we are not under the proverbial thumb of another country, we are under the attitude of many that we no longer need God. This could be a fatal error for this "One Nation Under God." I for one, though I am not the only one, am calling on everyone who reads this to pray for this "experiment" of democracy. Most nations cannot talk about the longevity that the United States has enjoyed. I want to see this beautiful experiment continue for my grandchildren and great grandchildren. It has been said, we are only as strong as our weakest link. I don't want to be the "weak link" that does not pray and fast for our nation.

Question: Have you read the freedom documents since you left high school? Might be time to read them again.

happy birthday, anna!

You, dear children, are from God and have overcome them, because the one who is in you is greater than the one who is in the world.

1 John 4:4 (NIV)

Today, I want to introduce you to one of the most courageous women I know, my friend Anna. Now she is not the kind of courageous that stands up to armed gunmen, though that is definitely courageous. She has never run into a burning building to save a child, though that would be very courageous. No, she is not even the courageous woman who would jump into a pool to save someone. She can't swim.

No, Anna epitomizes what I call a kind of "common sense" courageous. She was just a young girl in Poland when her mom died leaving an older sister who would take the place of her mother when her dad went to work. She also had a younger sister both sisters looked after. By the time Hitler invaded Poland in 1939 at the beginning of World War II, Anna was fourteen years old. As a family, they were mandated by law to place a list on the outside of their home describing who lived inside, including ages. One fateful day, the gestapo came to their home and took the girls each in a different direction. Anna didn't see her sisters or father after that day.

Her kidnappers took her to Germany. A farmer and his wife had no children and Anna became their housekeeper, cook, and animal caregiver. Apparently, this man was somebody important in the Nazi crime machine, and he received special help. Anna was treated very well there. She became like a member of the family and always had food and shelter. She cooked and cleaned for the family and often did chores on the farm. One of the chores was collecting eggs from the chickens each day. On occasion, the gestapo would stop by the farm to get their cut of the eggs. When this would happen, there would not be enough eggs for the family and the help to have breakfast. Anna was not about to let this happen! One day when she knew they would be stopping by, she had already taken all but a few of the eggs into the home and hid them. Of course, the gestapo realized there were more chickens than eggs and questioned this fourteen-year-old girl. Quick on her feet with an answer she told them, "Some of these are not chickens, but roosters. They do not lay eggs." Now this one statement could have sent her straight to a concentration camp or worse if the gestapo were smart enough to realize they were all chickens. What would make her do such a thing? Anna was a survivor! Since the gestapo didn't know how to prove her wrong, they chuckled at themselves, grabbed the eggs, and moved on. Anna continued doing that throughout her time on the farm. Very daring, but she chuckled as she told me. That was how Anna survived many awful situations. Many she would not even speak of because the horror was too great for her to re-live.

When the war finally ended, she returned to Germany. She met and married a German man, and they settled down to raise a family. Maybe things would be better now. Yet, her husband was determined to make a better life for them in the United States! The two of them traveled to the United States with two young girls. They settled in New Jersey and rented an apartment. Money was very tight, so Anna would help out by making all the girls' clothes, sewing for others, and even cleaning homes. She became very skilled at making friends who liked to help her. She took her family to church every Sunday and always trusted that God would provide for them, and He always did.

At some point, something like "welfare" was given to immigrants from war torn areas. Anna took care of the family bills. She received the "welfare" of course. Her neighbors were very generous to her with food and sometimes clothes or shoes for the girls. Her husband worked and got paid. One day, Anna told him it was time for them to get their own home. He questioned her about having enough money to buy a home. She said she had the money, and she did! She had been saving every penny she got from people, her job, and welfare living very frugally until she had enough saved to buy their American Dream home!

It was a home with two apartments. By this time, a boy was birthed into the family, and the oldest daughter got married and moved into one of the apartments. Often, the daughter and her husband struggled to pay the rent. Her husband wanted them to move if they could not pay. Anna, in her shrewd intelligence, gave her daughter the money to pay the rent. When her daughter went to give it to her dad to pay the rent, he could not take it from her! Once again Anna helped keep her family fed and sheltered.

Unfortunately, later in her life she was given a hard blow. Her husband passed away first. Then both her daughters died of cancer. She moved to Pennsylvania, where I met her and became her friend and her pastor's wife. She lived in her own apartment in her son-in-law's home. Later, two granddaughters and a grandson died from drug related problems. Anna lived on! Then, her son-in-law died. She had to move into a nursing home. I wondered what made her so resilient after so much tragedy in her life. I asked her. She answered in one word: Jesus!

Anna would have celebrated her ninety-fourth birthday in May 2020, but she went to be with her Jesus in 2019 at the age of ninety-three. She was truly a remarkable human being, and I learned so much from her. I will always be grateful for my Anna!

As we go through our own challenging times, let's not forget, it's only Jesus who will never leave us, and He will get us through.

Question: Is it Jesus you rely on when you are up against a struggle?

happy birthday, united states!

"No people can be bound to acknowledge and adore the Invisible Hand which conducts the affairs of men more than those of the United States."

George Washington

Blessed is the nation whose God is the LORD, the people he chose for his inheritance.

Psalm 33:12 (NIV)

Our grand old country is over 240 years old! That is a reason to celebrate with fireworks, picnics, parades, concerts, and more. I'm all in favor of allowing our national pride to be shamelessly demonstrated everywhere and by everyone in this great country with red, white, and blue everything, everywhere! Yes, I'm a patriot and still believe God isn't giving up on our nation. Why? Because there is a remnant praying earnestly for revival. I am one. I hope you are too.

The brilliant men who were at the helm of establishing this United States had to lean on a common understanding of law, social order, government, and morality. Where did they find that wisdom? It came from what we now call the "Judeo-Christian Ethic." This is the system that was found in the Old and New Testaments of the Bible. It was already tried, tested, and found to be true.

It was not as important that all the founders were Christians and lived as Christians, but it was critical that they lived by the code of ethics, and that they saw the value in these principles for this fledgling society. As it is, most were Christian believers, contrary to what some people express today.

So, what were these principles? I'm glad you asked. There are seven of them:

1. The Dignity of Human Life: "You shall not murder" (Exodus 20:13, NIV). Respect and protection for the born, and unborn. "And the second is like it: 'Love your neighbor as yourself'" (Matthew 22:39, NIV). Our military go to foreign lands to protect our neighbors.

2. The Traditional Monogamous Family: "The man said, 'This is now bone of my bones and flesh of my flesh; she shall be called "woman," for she was taken out of man.' That is why a man leaves his father and mother and is united to his wife, and they become one flesh" (Genesis 2:23-24, NIV). The plan of God, nature and common sense is one of each gender providing stability and nurturing for children without ambiguity. It is the only way life will go on.

3. A National Work Ethic: "For even when we were with you, we gave you this rule: 'The one who is unwilling to work shall not eat'" (2 Thessalonians 3:10, NIV). Even when the country went through the Great Depression, we as people helped each other until times got better. Often families sacrificed their own needs to help others.

4. The Right to a God-Centered Education: "Fathers, do not exasperate your children; instead, bring them up in the training and instruction of the LORD" (Ephesians 6:4, NIV). The early children's textbook *The New England Primer* taught the ABCs by having the children learn scripture verses with each letter of the alphabet. That was reading to believe in.

5. The Abrahamic Covenant: "The LORD had said to Abram, 'Go from your country, your people and your father's

household to the land I will show you. I will make you into a great nation, and I will bless you; I will make your name great, and you will be a blessing. I will bless those who bless you, and whoever curses you I will curse; and all peoples on earth will be blessed through you'" (Genesis 12:1-3, NIV). This was the decision made between Abraham and God that this promise would be kept between them; if Abraham would obey God and His commandments, God would bless Abraham with generations of children that would outnumber the stars in the Heavens. God kept His end.

6. Common Decency: "And the second is like it: 'Love your neighbor as yourself'" (Matthew 22:39, NIV). This is the belief that this "decent" nation will do the decent and good thing for its people when faced with an epic challenge.

7. Our Personal Accountability to God: "Just as people are destined to die once, and after that to face judgment," (Hebrews 9:27, NIV). Probably the greatest restraint to evil in this nation is the knowledge that we are accountable to God on judgement day. There will be a penalty for doing wrong and a blessing for doing what is right.

These seven principles are still effective today in keeping our nation safe and free. But it will only happen when we know them and heed them. Abraham Lincoln said, "We have been the recipients of the choicest bounties of Heaven." I pray and ask you to pray with me that our nation will return to these seven values and return to "One Nation Under God."

Question: Were you aware that our ethics have their roots in God's Word?

hosanna! praise him!

The crowds that went ahead of him and those that followed shouted, "Hosanna to the Son of David!" "Blessed is he who comes in the name of the LORD!" "Hosanna in the highest heaven!"

Matthew 21:9 (NIV)

Hosanna! Palm Sunday is a Sunday to celebrate! Our King comes into Jerusalem, facing what will be the worst week of His life.

Ever wonder how this crowd of faithful followers were so ecstatic on Sunday, turned against Him only a few days later? I wondered, then asked the Holy Spirit why? I was impressed to read the account of Matthew after the triumphal entry. Matthew 21 (NIV) describes such a beautiful scene. Here comes Jesus, the man who healed our diseases, opened our eyes to see and our ears to hear. Let's go rejoice. He is coming! They tore down palm branches and threw their coats on the ground to make a smooth path for the man who had done so much for them. Then he rode in on a donkey, a sign of peace. Maybe He can help me too?

I got this picture in my mind's eye: It was the week before Christmas in our little borough. Santa Claus rode through the streets on a firetruck. He was looking for children to give candy to and looking for their parents and grandparents to give donations to. For the children, it was an uproar of jubilation! Santa! Santa! Santa! This year, I watched as a small boy down the street was lifted up to sit next to Santa. The firetruck started moving down the street with the four-year-old still next to Santa! He got to my house, a few doors down, and the firetruck finally stopped. Mom was running down the street to get her little elf. Santa yelled to me, "He asked if he could come with me. I just didn't think he would." We both laughed and his mom grabbed him from the seat, and he cried! He wanted to go with Santa.

This little guy knew what Santa was about: toys! He was the guy who brought new stuff. This was the attitude of the people on Palm Sunday! I believe many in the crowd that day had a miracle in their lives. The blind man was healed. The lame man walked. The demoniac had demons removed and life restored. The blood disease was stopped. Many of those people were on the sidelines in this parade waving palms. Many others followed because they heard or saw these miracles, and they wanted one! Many others followed because, well, they wanted to see what all the excitement was about.

We are often no different than that crowd! We follow Jesus because we were healed, we heard of someone who was healed, or maybe even we just run alongside someone who saw something, and we are hopeful it will happen to us! However, when Jesus entered Jerusalem, the whole city was stirred! "Who is this?" The crowds answered, "This is Jesus the prophet from Nazareth in Galilee." They had an idea of who he was, but not really.

Immediately when Jesus entered the temple area, he showed another side of his divine nature. He became indignant with the way people were behaving in the temple, making it a type of "Wall Street." He took a whip and drove out the brokers.

He continued healing as he did before, but now the chief priests and teachers of the law challenged him. He answered with his own challenge in Matthew 21:16 (NIV). He spoke to them in several parables that would also challenge the way they lived. The truths he was giving them made them think, and they were not all happy looking at how their lives stacked up to his words.

We also follow when everything is going our way and life is good. But when we get some instruction we don't like, well, we may change churches, denominations, or stop going altogether. We are fickle people. We still have not learned.

Question: What am I following Jesus for?

laus deo

Praise be to God, who has not rejected my prayer or withheld his love from me!

Psalm 66:20 (NIV)

In our very secularized society where it appears that God and His Word have been erased from all our public buildings, God still shows up! There are many government buildings and monuments that still bear the words our nation was founded on. Today we will just take a look at the ones we can find in Washington, D.C. From the halls of Congress to the monuments and to nearly every landmark building, biblical and religious quotes and images are inscribed and preserved as a testimony to the true place God has in our nation's birth and history.

Just look up at the photo of the Washington Monument. Of course, you cannot read it up there, so we have to trust the ones who wrote it on this beautiful marble and aluminum obelisk, at the capstone, "Laus Deo," meaning "Praise be to God." On the blocks inside that line the stairwell are these phrases, "Holiness to the Lord," "Search the Scriptures," and "Train up a child in the way he should go, and when he is old he will not depart from it."

In the U.S. Capitol House Chamber is the inscription "In God We Trust." Also, above the gallery door stands a marble relief of Moses surrounded by twenty-two other lawgivers. In the rotunda are several paintings, including one of *The Baptism of Pocahontas* and one of the pilgrims praying on a ship. An open Bible can clearly be seen with the words "the New Testament according to our Lord and Savior Jesus Christ." Psalm 16:1 is etched in a window.

The Supreme Court building has many places where you can see Moses with the Ten Commandments. The one I find most interesting is on the huge doors as you enter the Supreme Court. The Ten Commandments are engraved on the lower part of each door. All the lawmakers entering that chamber each day must pass by God's laws! The Ten Commandments are also engraved over the top of Chief Justice Roberts' chair.

When you enter the Jefferson Memorial you will find many references to God. One of the panels reads, "God who gave us life gave us liberty. Can the liberties of a nation be secure when we have removed a conviction that these liberties are a gift from God? Indeed I tremble for my country when I reflect that God is just, that His justice cannot sleep forever." Apparently, Jefferson had some concerns about the condition of the country's Godliness even then.

Finally, the Lincoln Memorial has his famous speeches engraved on the walls. Both speeches have several references to God and quotes from the Bible.

Though many will try, they will not be able to expunge the Word of God from our government. The Bible says about itself, "the Word of God is quick and powerful," cutting in and cutting out (Hebrews 4:12, KJV). As a result, this nation will always be "One Nation Under God." In your travels go on a 'words of God' hunt. You may be surprised where you find them. Here's a good place to start looking, the Capitol Rotunda in Harrisburg, Pennsylvania.

Question: Have you already found some places that display God's Word?

memories...

For our struggle is not against flesh and blood, but against the rulers, against the authorities, against the powers of this dark world and against the spiritual forces of evil in the heavenly realms.

Ephesians 6:12 (NIV)

I was thinking about that old song from the movie *The Way We Were* with the same title. One of the verses says, "Memories light the corners of our mind." It's kind of a funny statement, yet true. Memorial Day is the day we set aside in this nation to remember our war dead. Even if that tragedy didn't come to knock on your door, you know someone or you can empathize with someone who has had this grief. The sad question I have is, are we remembering? Oh, we celebrate the day pretty well. The day off work, fireworks, picnics with family and friends, parades, wonderful patriotic music and shows, but is that the "memory that lights the corners of our mind?"

In 1971, Memorial Day became an official federal holiday observed on the last Monday in May. Previous to 1971, this day was set aside to decorate the graves and honor those who lost their lives in wars following the Civil War. Quite a somber occasion, I think.

Now we are still in the midst of a "war" of a different kind. A war with an invisible foe that has been attacking the United States with a steady decline in godliness. Just like every other war, there are deaths, many of them. But unlike other wars, there will be no peace treaty, armistice, or truce without a return to our foundational roots. This enemy cannot be negotiated to an end. It must be prayed over to reach the goal.

On Memorial Day, please remember all the men and women who gave their lives so we could have the freedoms we enjoy. Then, out of respect for them, give some very serious thought about how we lost some of those freedoms through other wars and conflicts over the years. I am hoping we will suffer no more loss, but only time will tell. If some legislators would have their way, even more would be taken from us, as their thought is, "we know what is best for you."

We need always to remember, our preamble says, "We the People." That's you and me. We the people pay their salaries. We the people have been surrendering to their superior knowledge, We the people vote them in or out!

Please allow every Memorial Day to "light the corners of your mind." Allow Memorial Day to remind you that Americans are not weak people who need to be told what to do. Many of the wars we fought included the knowledge that loss of life was a very real possibility. Yet, they forged ahead for the sake of our freedom. Now is not the time to drop our courage and pick up their propaganda! Now is the time to investigate for ourselves. Stand up for ourselves. Win the battle for us all!

A wise statesman once said, "we have nothing to fear, but fear itself." It's true. If we live in fear, we will die to fear.

Question: Is there a special celebration we could have to bring honor to our Memorial Day?

penn's woods

> But seek first his kingdom and his righteousness, and all these things will be given to you as well.
>
> Matthew 6:33 (NIV)

It's unfortunate that when I was in school, I felt like history was just a bunch of facts and dates to memorize. My history teachers didn't make the topic interesting either. Now, however, I see the value in knowing and understanding our history. I can't say I have mastered it, and I probably never will. But I can say I'm interested in it now because so much of our history came straight out of the Bible.

Take William Penn, for example. He was the founder of Pennsylvania and my grandmother always said when we would go on road trips, "These are Penn's Woods!" I didn't really know what that meant at the time, but now I say it myself as I look out at all our beautiful wooded areas in the state of Pennsylvania. I think about the man who made these wooded areas possible.

William Penn received much of "Penn's Woods" for payment of a debt that was owed to his father by King Charles II of England. All I can say is that was quite a debt! With the land in his possession, he envisioned a "holy experiment," an opportunity almost without parallel in human history. He had a humanitarian plan, not a selfish plan for his woods.

Penn, being a religious man, set out to set up his colony as a haven for religious freedom. He was advanced in his thinking for the times. When he set out the plan for the city of Philadelphia, he had open spaces, areas for fire protection, and of course areas that would be left wooded, undeveloped.

He treated the natives kindly, and he did not exploit them but respected them. He and his fellow Quakers told them about Jesus but sought not to convert them to Christianity, but rather to learn from the culture and religious beliefs of the natives.

Many of Penn's ideals were later found in the United States Constitution and the Bill of Rights. In fact, much of Penn's practices are very well known. What is not so well known is that much of his life and writings are Scripture oriented.

William Penn, founder of Pennsylvania, city planner, writer, Quaker, and friend to all. I can be proud to know that the commonwealth I live in today had its foundation in Word. Now that we know, we can pray that our leaders get back to the truth of God's Word as they govern "Penn's Woods."

> "I desire that I may not be unworthy of his love, but do that which may answer his kind providence, and serve his truth and people; that an example may be set up to the nations; there may be room there, though not here, for such an holy experiment."

William Penn, Governor of Pennsylvania

Question: Did you learn that William Penn was a Christian in your school? What else do you know about him?

presidential ponderings

All Scripture is God-breathed and is useful for teaching, rebuking, correcting and training in righteousness.

2 Timothy 3:16 NIV

Ever wonder what the President of the United States of America might be pondering? Well, you don't have to wonder with our current president, he pretty much vocalizes his thoughts on Twitter! Other Presidents did not have that luxury, but they did often write their thoughts down.

Would it surprise you that many of our presidents often read and quoted scripture? I would like to take this opportunity to just look at some of the quotes our president's and others made. Why do we want to know this? Well, in an age when we are told that we need "separation of church and state" you will clearly see that our past notable and quotable people did not believe it meant to take any helpful Bible scripture out of our speech and guiding principles.

From our Eighteenth president, U.S. Grant: "Hold fast to the Bible as the sheet anchor of your liberties. Write its precepts in your hearts, and practice them in your lives. To the influence of this book are we indebted for all the progress made in true civilization, and to this we must look as our guide in the future. Righteousness exalted a nation, but sin is a reproach to any people."

From our twenty-third president, Benjamin Harrison: "If you take out of your statues, your constitution, your family life all that is taken from the Sacred Book, what would be left to bind society together?"

From our sixteenth president, Abraham Lincoln: "In regard for this book I have this to say, it is the best gift God has given to man. All the good Savior gave to the world was communicated through this book."

From the seventh president; Andrew Jackson: "That book, sir, is the Rock on which our Republic rests."

From our first president, George Washington: "It is impossible to rightly govern the world without God and the Bible."

And finally, our current and forty-fifth president, Donald J. Trump: "We're going to protect Christianity. We don't have to be politically correct about it."

I for one, am encouraged by the fact that our president sees the value of involving Christianity in our nation. There is no other way to succeed.

In concluding this devotional, this is just a small slice of the thoughts and quotes our presidents have presented to the American people. Only God knows what is in the heart, but their clear intent was that God, the one and only Divine Creator of the universe, holds the United States in His mighty hands. And He is not about to let it go!

Question: Did it surprise you that so many of our presidents quoted scripture?

ruby—love

all in a day's work

> In the beginning you laid the foundations of the earth, and the heavens are the work of your hands.
>
> Psalm 102:25 (NIV)

Have you ever thought about how God actually made the universe? Oh, I know the narrative in Genesis, but that does not satisfy my curiosity. What are the mechanics of it? Did He have a blueprint? Was it just in His mind's eye? Since He existed before the rest of the physical world, how did He begin organizing a shapeless and barren earth into a habitable place for His crowning achievement mankind?

We recently purchased a "junior architect" kit for our grandsons. My husband taught architecture to junior high school students, and we thought they might be interested. I know I am. There are such interesting rulers, triangles, and other mechanical tools I have no experience using, but I would like to learn.

That is what I mean with God. Did He sit down at a drafting board and draw out all of the little details of the earth? Did he measure how big to make a whale so there would be enough room in the ocean for many whales? Did He use a protractor or French curve to be sure the valley and mountain would be correct? Did He have a color palette when He decided the colors of the butterflies, flowers, and birds?

Of course, all my ponderings are just that, ponderings. Until all is revealed to us in heaven, we will just be speculating these huge concepts. But God, with Jesus and the Holy Spirit, did it! Can you just imagine the Trinity establishing how the ocean tides would coincide with the sun and moon? Or how everything that was ever made has been made and will never be destroyed. How long did it take us mere humans to figure out these intricacies of the earth that we think we know?

He did it! It was all in a day's work for Him. Six days of creating, then a day for rest. Everything we are familiar with in this world was made in those six days. Nothing has been created that is new since then. He did it all; we cannot. We have everything we need.

Just ponderings. Our God is without a rival, no one comes close. Give Him praise!

Next time you go to work think about what God did in one day, you might want to work a little harder!

Question: Do you think we can still invent something new from what God has already created?

amadeo

He answered, "'Love the LORD your God with all your heart and with all your soul and with all your strength and with all your mind;' and, 'Love your neighbor as yourself.'"

Luke 10:27 (NIV)

I really enjoy listening to Christian music when I am working around the house. A fairly new song grabbed my attention, *Amadeo*. I don't know if you've heard it but it has a very catchy tune, and since the word "Amadeo" is repeated several times, well, it's just stuck in my head!

But what does it mean? I did some research and found that one word, means a lot! It's an Italian given name meaning "lover of God." Wow! Ryan Stevenson sings the song and the lyrics really speak to my heart, "You are still my God."

Once when a lawyer stood up and asked Jesus a question, Jesus threw the question back at him. Jesus asked him, "What is written in the law? What is your reading of it?" (Luke 10:26, NIV). The lawyer said, "you shall love the Lord your God with all your heart, with all your soul, with all your strength and with all your mind, and your neighbor as yourself" (Luke 10:27, NIV). This was the scripture that this lawyer would have known by heart from a child, yet he was asking Jesus. When Jesus said, "You have answered rightly, do this and you will live," the lawyer challenged Jesus by asking "and who is my neighbor?" (Luke 10:28-29, NIV).

Jesus then proceeds to tell the story of the Good Samaritan. We know how the wounded man was taken care of by the despised Samaritan. When Jesus asked who was the man's neighbor, the lawyer had to admit, "it was the one who had mercy on him" (Luke 10:36-37, NIV). The lawyer could not even say it was the "Samaritan."

I wonder, what would make someone do that for another human? Amadeo, lover of God. In our time, we hear of heroic measures of people saving others in floods, fires, or stranded by the side of the road. What makes them do it? Amadeo.

In the scripture, we are given a lot of instructions about what loving God really means. When we love God with our heart, we may have that feeling of love similar to what we have for a parent or grandparent. When we love God with our soul, this is on a spiritual level, maybe in prayer and worship. When we love God with our strength, we help a friend move, change a tire, paint a room. You get the picture. When we love God with our mind, we are only thinking thoughts of His Word and what it means in our lives. When He says, "and love your neighbor as yourself," now He is touching the very core of our being. This requires so much more from us than the rest of them, but it comes with great rewards as we can feel the approval of God, and you can claim, "Amadeo, I am a lover of God."

Being a lover of God is more than singing a song, going to church, praying. and worshiping, it's also the hard stuff. Loving our neighbor even when their dog barks all day, Amadeo. When they park in front of your home when you need the space, Amadeo. When their tree falls in your yard, Amadeo. When they play their music loud, Amadeo.

We hear the word in our head reminding us to be a "lover of God." Now allow that word to drop the fifteen inches into your heart. Next opportunity you have to be a good neighbor, remember, Amadeo!

Question: What is a hard thing for you to do that will portray "Amadeo?"

butterfly kisses

Let no debt remain outstanding, except the continuing debt to love one another, for whoever loves others has fulfilled the law.

Romans 13:8 (NIV)

In June 2020, after three months my husband and I were able to go out to a restaurant and sit inside to eat. Of course, there were restrictions because of the virus; we still had to walk in with masks, and we both had to sit on the same side of the booth, but we were inside! We had an enjoyable dinner, though it was awkward trying to speak to one another and look at each other and eat with elbows bumping and necks straining. I was feeling somewhat annoyed with this process. I mumbled to myself, "This is no fun." The dinner was yummy, the service was superb, and the bill was very reasonable. I even came home with half of my dinner for the future. As we left with our masks in place, my husband got into the car first and called to me, "Check out the butterfly on the ground."

I really like butterflies, and if there is a butterfly on the ground, it is not a good thing. They flit and flutter flying from one flower to another. They enjoy the sweet nectar from the most colorful flowers, pollinating as they go. They do not sit on a hot pavement next to a car.

I bent down to check out the butterfly. It was moving, so I gave it a little push, thinking it might start moving again. It didn't. I put my hand down near the head part and pushed again. It basically walked onto my hand. Next, it walked up my arm and onto my bright blue top. It would not fly away. It walked to my cheek and sat there a while until I figured out how to move it gently without smudging the color from the wing. I finally saw it. One of its wings was sliced into two pieces. When this happens, a butterfly can no longer fly, no longer get food, no longer live. I carefully studied this magnificent creature. It's primary function in life was to bring beauty and color to our world and of course carry pollen from one plant to another to share more beauty. I carried my new friend over to a nearby bush outside the restaurant and gently placed it there. I was thankful for the brief time I was able to enjoy this amazing creation God placed here just to bring color to our world and a smile to our face.

God is so out of this world with His creativity. There are over 20,000 species of butterflies. They live in virtually every country but Antarctica and in the arid desert. Their primary purpose is to look beautiful and bring joy to us whenever we are sulking about, well, anything!

Thank You, Lord, for creating these beautiful creatures and for the special one you sent to me when I needed a reminder of your "love."

Question: Has God sent you a special reminder lately that He loves you?

chosen!

> For he chose us in him before the creation of the world to be holy and blameless in his sight. In love he predestined us for adoption to sonship through Jesus Christ, in accordance with his pleasure and will.
>
> Ephesians 1:4-5 (NIV)

I can't even imagine the joy my nephew and niece were feeling the day they finally adopted four children! They had fostered these four sweet kids for about two years. Though they have two biological children, they felt they still had room in their hearts, and home for a couple more. However, when these four were presented to them as a package, they were hooked.

That is not to say there have not been trials. Any family has them. It is to say that when the birth mother selflessly put the needs of her children above the wants of her heart, she was able to relinquish them to their "forever family." An interesting twist in this story is that my niece and nephew still stay in touch with the birth mom, and she kind of has been adopted by them as well.

I am very proud of this little family! They are a living gospel to the world. They are able to love these four as their own flesh and blood. They receive love from the children in return.

Did you know that we also have been adopted? When God told the Jewish disciples to go to the Gentiles and tell them about the Jewish Jesus, we were allowed to be "grafted" into the Jewish lineage. In that one move toward Gentiles, God showed us when we receive Jesus, we receive the same inheritance and life with God in heaven. And all the comforts of having the Holy Spirit here with us on earth. Isn't that incredible?

Yet it's the same as my nephew's adoption of his children. When they all walked into the courthouse, only five of them had the same surname. When they walked out, all nine could claim that name as theirs.

In Christ's plan, we walk into the courthouse with the name "sinner, separated from God." With just the acceptance of Christ as our Savior, the judge drops the gavel and says, "Not guilty!" We become part and parcel of a new family with the name, redeemed, forgiven child of the King, son of God.

I doubt if any of the children were thinking of the inheritance they could receive when the time came. But, yes, they will be included in any inheritance. They also have the comfort of being part of a loving family they can rely on. So do we as king's kids! And we have an inheritance to look forward to as well. Life eternally in a place prepared for us to live forever with no sickness or sorrow, no death or tears. We have God's surname!

Question: Have you gone to the "judge" of your soul and have you been adopted into God's family? It's easy to do, no two year wait and all the benefits of our Heavenly Father begin immediately.

he's right there!

Then Jesus told them this parable: "Suppose one of you has a hundred sheep and loses one of them. Doesn't he leave the ninety-nine in the open country and go after the lost sheep until he finds it? And when he finds it, he joyfully puts it on his shoulders and goes home. Then he calls his friends and neighbors together and says, 'Rejoice with me; I have found my lost sheep.' I tell you that in the same way there will be more rejoicing in heaven over one sinner who repents than over ninety-nine righteous persons who do not need to repent."

Luke 15:3-7 (NIV)

When our boys were young, a favorite vacation spot was Wildwood, New Jersey. We had friends who owned a hotel there, so we would often go to their place for a week of fun in the sun. When we first began going to the Surfrider, we were pretty inexperienced beachgoers. One very sunny day on the beach, I was out there too long having too much fun and not paying attention to the beautiful red glow I was experiencing! It may have been because I had something else on my mind.

It was early afternoon, and the boys were playing on the sand. We were up further on dryer land. Before long, our oldest came walking back to the blanket by himself. I asked, "Where is your little brother?" His answer, "Right there." He was pointing to some obscure spot on the beach among many people sitting all over the beach. How was I to see a small four-year-old boy? I asked again, with a more emphatic voice, "Aaron, where is your brother?" He calmly stated again, "Right there," as he pointed to the ocean. I could feel anxiety rising!

I stood and searched where I was, no Eliot. I moved closer, holding my hand over my eyes to shield the sun, no Eliot. I ran back to the blanket and told my husband that I could not find our baby! He became engaged in the search. The worst thoughts were running through my head. I began quietly imploring God to show me where my baby was! With no time to lose, I went to the lifeguard and told him. In less time than it took for me to call Eliot again, I saw small flags going up on each lifeguard chair, indicating "lost child." As the reality of that set in, I began to panic! We described what Eliot was wearing and his size and hair color. Then we took Aaron and had him show us exactly where he left his brother. Of course, by now, he was disoriented, and he walked to an area that other children had claimed. The entire beach line looked like the place he left Eliot.

Finally, a lifeguard drove up with a dune-buggy rescue vehicle. My husband went with him, Aaron and I stayed back and searched. Now with a dune-buggy involved, my anxiety level was through the roof. But it wasn't long before a sand-covered, little boy with yellow hair and a big grin came walking toward me. I screamed, "Eliot! Hallelujah you are okay! Where were you?" He turned toward the beach sand and said, "Right there." I grabbed him with all my might, getting myself covered with the scratchy sand. He had no idea why I was acting this way. We did tell him later. Soon the dune-buggy returned, we had a joyful reunion, and all the flags went down!

I had a whole new appreciation for the story in Luke 15 (NIV) about the lost sheep. Of course, Jesus was referring to a "lost sinner." Someone who strayed away from the Godly path that God searched until that sinner returned to a relationship with the Father. I knew how I felt thinking of the possibility of Eliot being lost to the ocean waves. My heart hurts now even thinking of it, and he is a healthy thirty-nine-year-old! Imagine how Father God feels when one of us who knew Him turns and walks away. It's hard for me to believe that someone who had the comfort, care, and promise of heaven would walk away from it. It's the best deal anywhere ever.

This little anecdote of a day at the beach comes back to me when I hear of people who make the choice to walk away from God. I wonder, what are they walking too? If you have walked away, it's not too late to turn around and walk back. He waits with arms wide open and no questions asked. Even if you are soiled and sandy, He wants you back! It's easy. Just look, He's "right there."

Question: Have you strayed from your first love of God? He's right there.

hi nana!

Evening, morning and noon I cry out in distress, and he hears my voice.

Psalm 55:17 (NIV)

My messenger notification was buzzing. Since I just started down the path with this new-to-me technology, I was not sure what to expect. To my happy surprise it was my third grandchild, seven-year-old, Grant. He and his family were at the shore, and he wanted to give me a "tour" of the apartment they were in for the week. We had a lovely chat, him showing me the rooms, me cooing over how beautiful the place is. I had several more questions about their plans for the week, and how his "brudder," Preston, was enjoying the place. Finally, he told me they were going to the boardwalk to ride their bikes. I want to get a "fuffle cake." He still has no front teeth and his Ns come out Fs. I chuckled and agreed that "fuffle" cakes are awesome on the boards. He called me daily, giving me the rundown on the activities the day before and the plan for that day. Just that call did a couple things for my day: first, of course, I got to communicate with one of my favorite people in the world; second, I knew how to pray for them for safety and fun for that day. It was a great plan, and I think it kept him occupied while his parents were getting all the other equipment ready for the day. Win-Win!

Sometimes it would be nice if God had a little reminder buzzer for us. It takes some discipline to get up early enough to have time to "catch up" with God before we run to the busyness of our day. But I do believe we get the same two benefits from our morning conversations with God, also known as "prayer time," when we commit to making that time a priority. First, we get to communicate with the one and only creator of the universe! That is mind boggling. Yet He says He wants to talk with us as much as we want to talk with Him. Remember, He came and talked with Adam and Eve in the cool of the evening?

Second, He hears right from us what is on our mind. What our plans are and where we need His help, advice, or even intervention. Of course, He knows these situations already, but just like our earthly fathers, He likes to hear it from us rather than just do what He does best: provide for His kids. It's another win-win situation. When we make this conversation our priority in our day, we are telling God, "You are important to me." I really feel that way when Grant calls me. He has friends he can call, even other things he could be doing, but he makes time to call and give me the news. I am important to him. We have an assurance that we have an all-powerful, all-knowing God working on our behalf with our specific requests. How can we go wrong?

Question: Have you called your Heavenly Father and said "Hi Dad!" Make His day and yours.

humble love: maundy thursday

Jesus replied, "You do not realize now what I am doing, but later you will understand." "No," said Peter, "you shall never wash my feet." Jesus answered, "Unless I wash you, you have no part with me."

John 13:7-8 (NIV)

Maundy Thursday. This is not a description that we use much anymore to describe the Thursday before Resurrection Day. "Holy Thursday" has become more popular. But Maundy describes what our Savior did on that day, as we will see.

Let's backup a minute. As the Passover was approaching, Jesus told his disciples to find a venue for their feast. "Go into the city to a certain man and tell him, 'The teacher says: My appointed time is near. I am going to celebrate the Passover with my disciples at your house.'" (Matthew 26:18, NIV).

When everything was prepared and Jesus was ready with his disciples to recline and eat the meal, Jesus knew this would be the last meal with the people he had poured most of his live into over the last three years. Was it enough? Did he get through? He wanted to show them the full extent of his love for them before the cross. He took off his outer garment and wrapped a towel around his waist. He poured water into a basin and began washing the disciple's feet and dried them with the towel he had wrapped around him. Hence the term "Maundy," it means "foot washing."

This was an extremely significant act of servanthood, humility, and love. The roads were parched and dusty from no rain. The dust that settled on their feet would be very uncomfortable, and since they reclined when they ate, their feet would be in close proximity to the next person. A servant in a home usually greeted guests with a basin of cool water and a towel so they could refresh their feet. Jesus humbled himself and became a servant, showing them what they should be doing as his followers.

As the meal began, he predicted that one of them would betray him. Of course, they all denied it, but he was already aware of who the traitor was. Even Judas denied it by saying, "'Surely, you don't mean me, Rabbi?' Jesus answered. 'You have said so'" (Matthew 26:25, NIV).

They continued with their very meaningful Seder dinner. This is where Jesus instituted the "Lord's Supper," or Communion. It was another beautiful presentation to them of what he was about to do for them and us. In Matthew 26: 26-29 (NIV), Jesus told his disciple to eat this bread and drink this cup as it is a covenant of forgiveness of sins, He told them he would not eat or drink with them again until they were in his Father's Kingdom. Did they understand? Probably not. Like talking to someone who already knows the end of a movie you have not seen, they sat in the dark, befuddled by his words. He was grieving already for their spirits. He knew he would be leaving them behind. Were they ready? Yet can you every really know if you are ready to deal with a life changing event before it occurs? Nothing can really prepare you for marriage, or a baby, or even a new job, no matter how much you learn. All the talks they had about this one event didn't prepare them for what they would do, even that night.

But Jesus knew what they would do! He told them, "This very night you will all fall away on account of me, for it is written: I will strike the shepherd, and the sheep of the flock will be scattered" (Matthew 26:31, NIV).

Again, they denied it. But the Bible tells us, "the heart is deceitful above all things and beyond cure. Who can understand it?" (Jeremiah

17:9, NIV). We don't even know what we will do in these most stressful of times. Of course, we know Peter denied Jesus later that evening after Jesus was arrested. We also know many of the disciples dispersed, some even turned away. But those who remained or returned evangelized pretty much all of the known world at that time. On foot or donkey, by ships. No hotels, no phones, no bathrooms or showers. No toilet paper! They knew they had a message to die for. And most of them did.

Maundy Thursday is love humbled and personified in a simple carpenter who, with his twelve rag-tag followers, turned the world upside down. In the death of one everyone is offered eternal life.

Question: Knowing the end of this story, how do you imagine you would have responded? Can you really know for sure?

i hate...

Love must be sincere. Hate what is evil; cling to what is good. Be devoted to one another in love. Honor one another above yourselves. Never be lacking in zeal, but keep your spiritual fervor, serving the LORD. Be joyful in hope, patient in affliction, faithful in prayer.

Romans 12:9-10 (NIV)

That title is a tough statement for a believer who is not supposed to hate! Yet Paul tells us in Romans 12:9 (NIV), "hate what is evil." How do we know if something is evil? Can we trust our own hearts to know? Not always. Remember the Bible tells us in Jeremiah 17:9 (NIV) our hearts are deceitful! We can trust the Word of God, the scriptures, and the Holy Spirit to give us guidance.

One of the first things we can do is take the word "hate" right out of our vocabulary. We use it so carelessly I am not sure we even hear ourselves or think about its meaning. I hate when it rains, I hate my hair, I hate bologna sandwiches. While these are all inanimate objects and it does not hurt them to hate them, it does hurt you! Words are not just words. When spoken out loud, they reinforce your thoughts and feelings about something. When we say and feel hate, we are allowing it to stir around inside our emotional think tank. Just like any other emotion it begins to color our feelings with that rotten hate color! Soon it spills over into our actions and on to other people!

There is a way to take that color right out of your emotional color palette. The same scripture that tells us not to hate, tells us what to do" do good.

By the way, the scripture says hate *what* is evil not *who* is evil. Hating someone for whom Christ died is *never* an option. We may feel that the evilest person we can think of deserves to be hated. God doesn't and still offers redemption to them. So should we. Is it easy? No. Do you think it was easy to watch as God's son died for you? No. But He did it. and with His help, we can love them too!

Try to pay close attention to your speech this week. See how often the word "hate" enters your conversation. Once you become aware of it, you can swap it out with another word that does not carry the volatility of the hate word. You might use different descriptive words, stretch your vocabulary. There is a plethora of adjectives for how you feel about something. Use a thesaurus if needed.

So, even the evil Darth Vader should not be hated. Remember he was once Anakin and had a great ability to love. We need also to love and be devoted to each other. See the "Anakin" in everyone you meet. That's how God sees them, remember, that's how God sees you!

Question: Is there someone you feel hatred toward? Go to God and work it out.

up, up, and away!

Since, then, you have been raised with Christ, set your hearts on things above, where Christ is, seated at the right hand of God.

Colossians 3:1 (NIV)

There is an overwhelming feeling we get when our hearts are connected with another person! In the movie *Bambi*, Thumper called it "twitterpated." We might call it love, but not always in the sense of lovers. I know you have felt it in your lifetime! It's this feeling: You popped the question or had it popped to you, and if you had been waiting for it and imagining when it would happen, you are twitterpated! As you are standing waiting for your bride to enter the church and walk down the aisle, your heart skips a beat in anticipation, then she enters, and you are beside yourself with joy.

Or the doctor announces, "You have a healthy baby girl" or "You have a healthy baby boy." You react with awe and your entire being rises for the occasion. Or your oldest makes the honor roll for the first time and your spirit soars. Or your youngest makes the basket that wins the game. Oh yeah, you are soaring!

Or maybe you just gave your heart to Jesus and promised to give your entire future to Him. The burdens of this life lift, and you feel like you are so light you can just float into the atmosphere! That's what Jesus is reminding us in today's scripture verse. After all, He said our eternal dwelling place is in Heaven with Him!

Let's talk about that for a minute. When our heart is set on something, we have this idea that we will do that thing or get that thing. I have my heart set on a sapphire anniversary ring. Sapphire is the gemstone for the forty-fifth anniversary. June 2020 is ours! So, I have been stopping in every jewelry store at the mall, checking things out online, looking at my friend's rings for ideas. My heart is set on that ring!

We have some changes in our attitude when our heart is set on something. Before we were thinking of marriage when our friends got engaged, it was great for them, but we were not twitterpated. We may have been to many weddings, and the excitement of seeing the bride for the first time has you camera ready, but you are not beside yourself with joy. Oh sure, we always enjoy births, but nothing beats the voice of the doctor with the announcement of *your* child, and no other child is as beautiful as yours! Your entire being is in awe.

You get the picture. These are all wonderful occasions, just not *your* occasions. Yet, when you receive Jesus into *your* heart, when you have asked for forgiveness and said you will follow His lead, well, then you have *your* mind set on things above. Since it's you and your heart, it is so much more remarkable. It is *your* occasion. It is *your* life that has changed. It is you that has a place being prepared for you in the most glorious place in the universe, heaven! From now on, your heart will be set on Jesus, and what He desires for your life. Of course, your emotions and thoughts will be raised with Christ. And when you have been raised with Christ, well, you know what they say, "a rising tide lifts all boats." Be the "rising tide" that lifts all boats to set their hearts on Jesus!

Question: Can you remember the exact day you set your heart on Jesus for the first time?

yummy marinade recipe

Blessed is the one who does not walk in step with the wicked or stand in the way that sinners take...but whose delight is in the law of the LORD, and who meditates on his Law Day and night. That person is like a tree planted by streams of water, which yields its fruit in season and whose leaf...Not so the wicked! They are like chaff that the wind blows away.

Psalm 1: 1-4 (NIV)

I pierced the last couple holes into the steak I was marinating in my secret sauce. It looked like it was going to be perfect for our dinner after sitting in those yummy juices for most of the day. The new air fryer would cook it up just right. My secret sauce recipe was an idea from the recipe book that came with the air fryer, then I added ingredients of my own. We seemed to be using the same combinations of spices all the time so trying a new recipe was an experiment in new cooking territory. Well, it became a happy accident, and I have used it many times since then, on several kinds and cuts of meats.

I went back to my Bible reading and prayer time. I heard the Lord telling me, "I want you to marinate with me as your 'secret sauce.' I want you to soak my rich goodness, my wisdom, and especially, my love. It is after you have been in my presence soaking that you will be tender, useful and flavorful to do my work." It was startling to me. Was the Lord really saying I should "marinate?" Yes. Yes, He was! Remember when Jesus was here how He used visual aids to capture the attention of the people and then keep their attention. When they were back out in their world and that particular item came into view, they remembered that particular lesson Jesus taught them. Remember, for the most part they were unschooled peasants that came to hear Jesus. They had no ability to take notes for their future study. Their memory was their best friend. We know how reliable that can be. But if there was an item they saw, used in their daily activity, touched in their work, well, that would be a powerful reminder of what the Master Teacher had been hoping to infuse into their spirits.

We are no different today. Sure, we are more educated, more sophisticated, more self-reliant, but we still rely on visual aids to remember what we need to remember. Before modern technology, we would tie a string around our pinkie to remember something important. Of course, that only worked if we remembered what the silly string was supposed to remind us! Now we have post it notes, notes on our phones, reminder alarms on our phones, and more. Jesus simply used bread, salt, mud, fish, and others. When I listed those items you probably can remember the stories He told that the item represented. Can you remember your pastor's sermon from last week without looking at your notes? Thought so! Clearly a tangible object we can see and touch is a better reminder.

So, back to my marinade. When we take the time to "marinate" in the Lord on a regular basis, we become tender to Him. When we become tender to Him, we become tender to those with needs around us. When we become tender to those needs, we are prompted to do something. When we do something, we are behaving like a Christian Ambassador. And not only an ambassador but one who is tasty, loveable, and easy to be believed and accepted. Certainly not that tough critical person we were before marinating in the secret sauce of the Holy Spirit.

Question: Are your conversations a little tough lately? Are you spending time marinating in God's Word, talking to Jesus, listening to the Holy Spirit? Maybe it's time for some secret sauce marinating!

"Donna's Secret Sauce":

½ c. paprika

3 tbsp ground cayenne pepper

¼ c. freshly ground black pepper

¼ c. plus 2 tbsp garlic powder

3 tbsp onion powder

¼ c. salt

2 ½ tbsp oregano

2 ½ tbsp thyme

This makes enough for several uses. I store mine in a pint canning jar. When you are ready to use it, pierce your beef only, and rub on chicken parts. Then I place in a glass dish with apple cider vinegar and olive oil, covering lower portion of the meat. Soak a few hours, turn meat so the other portion is in the vinegar and oil and sprinkle seasoning on this half. Cook as usual. Yummy!

sapphire—faithful

1975

But Ruth replied, "Don't urge me to leave you or to turn back from you. Where you go I will go, and where you stay I will stay. Your people will be my people and your God my God."

Ruth 1:16 (NIV)

It was a beautiful spring day way back in 1975. Sunny, hot, not a cloud in the sky, perfect for a wedding. The bride and groom were as prepared as anyone really is for this life-changing event. They were young, in love, and looked as perfect as any two people could as they faced their day.

They moved into their apartment with great expectations that life would be perfect now that they were facing it together. It was summer vacation for him, a schoolteacher. She was laid off, so they had their entire summer together to set up house. They decorated, arranged and re-arranged furniture, tried new recipes, and explored their new neighborhood. They enjoyed getting to know each other. They were so in love!

Too soon, fall was approaching. He worked in a district that never had a strike until that year! Her unemployment was running out. Their first challenge was paying bills with little to no income. The Lord provided meals from the gardens of friends, take-home food from parents when they went there for dinner Sunday. Miraculously, bills all got paid. They never really figured out how it happened. Soon teachers were back to work, and the bride got a job as a teacher-aid in a day care.

A year or so later, great news exploded in their home: a baby was on the way! The news filled their hearts with joy and dreams for their little one. Their joy was short lived as the pain she had one day gave way to a miscarriage. She was hospitalized; he cried! While he was very upset about losing their baby, he was devastated about the prospect of losing her!

They went on together, not sure if a baby would be a reality for them, but they would face it together. They only waited six months for the miraculous news, and this time, the news of another pregnancy grew into a perfect boy!

By now, they had bought a fixer-upper home of their own and enjoyed painting, papering, cleaning, and getting the nursery just right for their little prince. God was good to them, and even though another miscarriage would again crush their dreams, another boy came along soon afterward. Two boys, one yard, one dog, one cat, one joyful family of love, and a fun place to play and run and grow!

There would be many more hurdles for this couple to navigate. Another move, or two, a flood, death of two parents, family problems, money problems, health problems. Every hurdle was successfully jumped, with the Lord's help. After each hurdle, the couple was a little closer, a little wiser, and a little more prepared to face the next one.

Many years and moments have transpired since that wedding day: June 14, 1975. The boys are grown and have their own families and children. The couple still faces, together, the hurdles that still come. The joys, however, drown out the sorrow. It's a good life.

So, this year they will face new joys! Milestones of their grandchildren. Their first is graduating from high school, and she is planning a career in teaching. The second in going into middle school, and he loves math and science. The third is going into second grade and is a thinker. And the youngest is off to kindergarten and has the only sports ability among them.

This family is probably not so different from many families. When you begin the journey, it often feels overwhelming. It may seem like the struggle is too great or you will never make it, you will! Our Lord never leaves us, always walks beside us, and in the darkest times, He shines His light on our path so we can see the next step.

I look around at other couples, some have had it easier, some way harder. Always, the common core of all who stick together is the commitment they have to each other. The verse above, from Ruth 1:16 (NIV), refers to the relationship between a mother-in-law and daughter-in-law. The bottom line is the same: commitment. That kind of commitment takes making a head choice that overrides a heart emotion. Emotions change day-to-day with each circumstance they face. Commitment stays when everyone else runs.

If you have not guessed already, I am talking about my own marriage. My husband and I celebrated our forty-fifth wedding anniversary in June 2020. I just thank the Lord every day for a marriage that has stood the test of time. A marriage with Christ at the center and His will our greatest desire. I love you Ron!

Question: If you are in a marriage relationship, what are the hurdles you have overcome with the Lord's help? If you are not in a marriage yet, what are the attributes you would like to see in a spouse. Do you see them in you?

don't pray about it

As soon as you began to pray, a word went out, which I have come to tell you, for you are highly esteemed. Therefore, consider the word and understand the vision.

Daniel 9:23 (NIV)

Well, that's not something you hear often, well, maybe you don't ever hear it! I know people who pray about everything, I mean everything! What clothes to wear, what food to eat. I always thought that was a little extreme, but I could be wrong. Yet there is a lot of truths to be investigated here. I mean, there are so many truths already listed in the Bible that you just need to walk in and trust. The prayer and waiting are already done for you. God is always for you, not against you. So, let's look at some of the situations you need to walk in, shall we?

Love your neighbors. New neighbors? Old neighbors with a noisy dog or car? No need to pray about it: love them. "The second is this: 'Love your neighbor as yourself.' There is no commandment greater than these" (Mark 12:31, NIV).

Giving. Do you see someone who needs something, and you have two of those somethings? No need to pray about that. Give and it will be given back to you. "Give, and it will be given to you. A good measure, pressed down, shaken together and running over, will be poured into your lap. For with the measure you use, it will be measured to you" (Luke 6:38, NIV).

A need surfaces in the body of Christ, meet it! No need to pray, just do it! "Therefore, as we have opportunity, let us do good to all people, especially to those who belong to the family of believers" (

Galatians 6:10, NIV).

Sometimes we get a case of "spiritual procrastination." We pray, hesitate, lose the opportunity, reprimand ourselves, repeat. We need to "nudge the needle" in our thinking. Remember vinyl records and the record player? At times, the needle would get stuck in a groove and would repeat the same phrase over and over until we physically went to the machine and gave the needle a nudge. I think our thinking needle needs a nudge at times! We get stuck in a rut of our own doing. Are we praying about it? Yes, but do we always need to pray about it, or does the Word already address it and we just need to re-visit the scriptures? Or have we already prayed about it and we continue to pray because we doubt God's answer?

When it comes to prayer, I do know the Lord loves to hear our prayers and stores them up for us and, of course, answers them. Please do not take this post in the wrong way. I am just imploring you, look at the circumstances. If the answer is in the Word already, just walk in it. If you have prayed about it, trust God. He did hear. He will answer in His time. Don't become a victim of "spiritual procrastination!"

Question: Has "spiritual procrastination" immobilized you? "Nudge your needle" and get moving. Time is running out.

exposed

Everyone who does evil hates the light, and will not come into the light for fear that their deeds will be exposed.

John 3:20 (NIV)

Many years ago, when our children were in elementary school, we lived in a larger city. We liked having neighbors so close and made friends with many of them. My mother-in-law eventually moved into an apartment we built over our detached garage. Behind her was an alley, I'm not even sure if they have these anymore in new developments, but we enjoyed ours. That is where the boys learned how to ride their bikes. They often played ball back there with friends, and they were always in our sight. The problem was, when the sun went down, it became a hang-out for teens!

They smoked back there, and the scent wafted up to my mother-in-law's windows. In the summer, she would have the windows open for the breeze, and it was spoiled by the teens' careless smoking and their loud, raucous, and often foul mouths!

She would tell us about this, and we would hear it as well. It did not take long before she started closing her windows and missing out on the summer breeze she loved! We started praying about it. The verse above came into my mind, and the Holy Spirit quickened an idea in me.

I called my mother-in-law and my neighbor. I told them when the crowd gathered that night in the alley, put all your outside lights on. We did! That bunch of teens never scattered so fast!

Scripture says it: evil has a fear of the light (John 3:20, NIV)! It's so true. That was just a simple illustration of this enormous Biblical truth. There is no fear of the glaring light of day if your deeds are good, but, if your deeds are evil, you prefer the dark. It's at night that people slink around in neighborhoods looking for mischief, and usually find it, or make it!

Having a similar problem around your home? Light your lights. Ever notice that businesses keep a light on? It's not only so people can see their way safely in the dark; it's so the ones doing the wrong things can be identified.

Question: Do you prefer to "be in the dark?" Are your deeds questionable? Or do you prefer the light of day where the fresh air of truth can light your pathway? Think about it.

frigid to fire!

"For in him we live and move and have our being." As some of your own poets have said, "We are his offspring."

Acts 17:28 (NIV)

In the Pocono Northeast, we can experience some pretty frigid temperatures. You know what I mean. The kind of temperatures that take your breath away as soon as you walk out the door. Temperatures that seem to pinch your nostrils together until they burn. The kind of temperatures that chill you-until you think the marrow in your bones is really turning to ice and your legs are too heavy to move!

When I sat in my "prayer chair" one day to have my devotional time, I felt that kind of cold in my own prayer room! I usually come to my devotional chair with great expectations for a time of comfort and revelation with my Lord. That day, however, I felt ice cold!

Determined to have my quiet time of Bible reading, study, and prayer anyway, I sat and closed my eyes in prayer. Beginning by thanking the Lord for all He has provided, I went down my list of blessings: health, home, provisions, family, etc. The room began to get warmer. I continued by reading in Psalms, "yea though I walk through the valley of the shadow, I fear no evil, for You are with me" (Psalm 23:4, NKJV). It's getting warmer! Then as I had a chat with my Heavenly Father, I felt His presence, and my frozen bones melted. My breathing slowed, and I could take deep breaths again.

I was reminded of a trip I took to Balboa Island, California. I sat on the sea wall, and the sun was shining down on my hair. It's warmth on the back of my neck permeated every part of my being. I was truly warmed inside and out, and I felt like a kid running around on the sandy shore, waves splashing noisily on my legs.

My enthusiasm splashed on to everyone I met that day. Absorbing those warm rays from the sun not only energized me for the moment, but that warm glow lasted long after the sun went down.

That was what I experienced that day I sat to pray with a chilled heart, but as I sat with Jesus, I was absorbing the warmth and glow of the Son. I stood up with a new attitude and a childlike faith after sitting with the Triune God. It made all the difference.

When we enter the Lord's presence in prayer and thanksgiving, an unexplained transformation happens in our heart and our mood. The day is warmer, brighter, and conquerable!

Question: Are you feeling chilly today? Go to the Son and be warmed and filled as only He can do!

gps: God's protection system

Now may our God and Father himself and our LORD Jesus clear the way for us to come to you.

1 Thessalonians 3:11 (NIV)

It's so exciting when you are planning to have company at your home! Getting to see friends and family you enjoy is one of the pleasures of life: connecting with those we love. Even the preparation is a fun event as you plan and prepare special meals, get rooms ready, and maybe plan to go to special places.

But just imagine what that might have looked like back in Bible times. With no plumbing, no extra bedrooms for most people, no grocery store trips, donut shops, or rental cars. Imagine the letter delivery system. The mule gets stubborn, and you get the letter guests are coming the day before they arrive! Needless to say, this would make any hostess/host a little anxious! In today's scripture passage, Paul tells the Thessalonians he is asking for God and Jesus to clear the way for him to get there for a visit. Why would Paul need to ask God and Jesus to clear the way? Let's explore this.

Paul had already met these people, the Thessalonians. It appears they built a bond over the time he was with them, and he wanted to go back to see how they were doing in their newfound faith in Jesus (1 Thessalonians 3, NIV). Paul began his plan for the trip by asking God Himself, and Jesus, to clear the way for them. These days, we have GPS systems to tell us if there is road construction, accidents, detours, or any other obstruction to our path. Back in Bible times, they had to rely on the best GPS system: prayer to God and Jesus! Remember, Jesus did tell us to ask Him whatever we want, and He will answer it (Jeremiah 33:3, NIV).

In Paul's case, he probably didn't need to worry about construction or accidents as much as robbers and powers of darkness that were seemingly lurking on every wilderness path: people who were desperate for food or water, demons who lived among the rocks hidden from passersby, or traveling caravans with nothing better to do. Even leper colonies who were to close as Paul went by. Did he himself bring enough provisions for the trip? There would be no gas station or convenient store anywhere on this road! We cannot begin to imagine the hindrances Paul and his friends might have encountered along the way if they were not prayed up! For more accounts of hindrances, read Luke 10:30-37 (NIV) and Daniel 10:12 (NIV).

So, here's the thing. Since anything can happen to anybody anytime and anywhere, turn on your GPS (God's Protection System) before you leave home. Ask God to clear your path of any issues before you leave the driveway! We do, and God has always been faithful.

Question: Can you recall a time when God divinely protected you because of prayer?

just ask me!

Call to me and I will answer you and tell you great and unsearchable things you do not know.

Jeremiah 33:33 (NIV)

Wondering, pondering, thinking, figuring. These are all favorite pastimes we share on those days when our work is caught up, the spring breeze is blowing, and we are feeling lazy. But what about those days when we really need to know something, and we need to know it now? The urgency is weighing down on you like a heavy blanket. How will I pay for this car repair? Where should I go to college? Whom should I marry? Should I marry at all? Where did I leave my phone? You may laugh at that last one, but sometimes the simple things cause us the most stress.

I have today's scripture verse memorized for times like these. You can count on God, through the manifest presence of the Holy Spirit, to give you the answer through any number of ways. I implore you to look back at your life and see if there were times you did not know what way to turn. Did you send up a prayer for help and direction in your situation? I know I did!

Over the years, I have experienced many situations where I have called out to God to tell me where to find things I could not find, mostly my phone or glasses! But I have also asked, "How can I pay this bill?" That particular question was asked when my husband was on strike with no pay, and I was laid off from my job. We were doing okay meeting most of our obligations, but it finally became apparent that our bills were just too big for our small resources.

We cried out to God for supernatural help, reciting this verse over and over. Well first, my husband received a call from a high school he was scheduled to do a seminar for in six months. They asked if they could pay him now as it was better for their bookkeeping system. Of course, he said yes! That covered a little less than half of the bills. The next day, I watched my friend's three children while she went on a day trip. It was a favor, not a business arrangement. Yet, when her husband returned and took over, he gave me a very generous check! Now we were even closer to meeting our obligations.

We went to church on Wednesday evening. A fairly new congregant poked my husband in the back and handed him an envelope. The man later told us that he received an unexpected check from his workplace. He called them and said, "You don't owe me any money. What's the check for?" After they researched it, they realized it was a mistake. But the company didn't want it back because it would mess up their books! This generous man said, "I could not keep it. It was not meant for me." When we got home my husband opened the envelope. In it was a check for the exact amount we needed to pay the rest of our bills!

Call on Him. He always answers, never puts you on hold, and you never get a busy signal.

Question: When you were at the end of yourself, how did God answer you?

listen!

But whoever listens to me will live in safety and be at ease, without fear of harm.

Proverbs 1:33 (NIV)

Let's go back in time a little. I mean all the way back to the 1960s. Remember those little transistor radios that every kid had to have? I had a red one! Then, when our parents got tired of hearing all the doo-wop music, they got us ear buds. Who knew that we would all be buying hearing aids now? Well, maybe the hearing aid inventor, just kidding.

Remember it was difficult at times to find the right bandwidth? Even though the bandwidth was always there, we needed to "fine tune" our search on the dial to get the station we wanted. I worked at a radio station for a while. It was a very low budget operation so, when we had winds or storms of any kind, the equipment would malfunction. Someone would physically need to go outside into some kind of a connector and realign the system. It wasn't me! So glad for the technology we have today.

Even today we need to tune that radio station to the right frequency to be able to listen to our favorite tunes. If you have a desire to hear from God, you need to "tune in" as well. All the white noise of the media, well-meaning friends and family will not bring you to the sweet spot on the bandwidth to hear from God. While He is always there, waiting, it is us who become distracted by all the stuff around us.

When we finally got the station we wanted, remember how rewarding it was to hear "our song?" Remember how the chorus would run around in our head for the rest of the day? Think about what our day can be like if that verse above runs around in our head all day? With the ever-present reminder of our safety, ease, and no fear, we could relax and enjoy the blessings God provides, counting on Him to keep us safe.

We live in a time of turmoil right now. Weather patterns are in an uproar as well as racial tensions. Not to even mention the risk to our health with a virus. We don't really know if or when the enemy will turn on us. In my son's area, they recently had a derecho, a powerful windstorm without the funnel of a hurricane. The week before, they had rioters a few blocks away trying to break into Macy's. These times are uncertain, to say the least.

So how do we tune into God's bandwidth to avail ourselves of God's promises? You got it, spend time with Him! I am sure you remember how long it took to adjust that radio to just the right frequency. Then we would move three feet away, and it would be gone. The process would start again. We were willing to put in the time to get the station and song we wanted. How badly do we want to hear what God has to tell us? Enough to spend some time listening for His voice in the crazy white noise all around us? If you take the time to tune in to God, you will find His bandwidth has always been there and will always be there. We need to spend the time to tune in. The tune from God is always our favorite: safety, ease in living, and no fear!

Take some time to "tune in" to God's bandwidth today!

Question: What "bandwidth" are you listening to? Does it lift you up or leave you lost?

looking in the rear-view mirror

Do your best to present yourself to God as one approved, a worker who does not need to be ashamed and who correctly handles the word of truth.

2 Timothy 2:15 NIV

I don't think it is a good idea to constantly look in the rear-view mirror while driving your car or living your life. When we do that, our memories become greater than our dreams. That's when we are headed for the grave. Sometimes, however, it is nice to look back and see how far we have come.

Recently, I watched a show that featured several Christian singing artists from forty years ago. This was when the Christian music genre was really making a big splash on the scene. I remember I had albums by many of these artists: Amy Grant, Michael W. Smith, Larnelle Harris, Russ Taff, Stephen Curtis Chapman, and Sandi Patty. These and many others were on the show. As they came out and sang their hits from the 1980s, I nearly cried! It just brought me right back to a simpler time in my life and in our nation. I felt like I lived my life right along with them. I had two young boys at the time. We were very active in our church, and the boys would hear this great array of gospel music in our home, in the car, and anywhere else we could play it.

Music penetrates our minds and hearts with a message. What message we choose is ours to make by the music we choose. We can choose music that is just a nonsense melody and word combination. Harmless, neutral in its effects. Just fun. We can choose songs that have messages that motivate us to be or do something. Maybe something good, maybe not! Or we can choose lyrics to songs that uplift us and motivate us to do what is right in God's eyes. These people listed, and so many more, do just that. They didn't come out proclaiming they are the shining example of what a Christian should be. Most of them had their struggles and pain. What they did do, for my home, was make the way and my day a little brighter, a little more pleasant and gave me an alternate music to listen to. Something that would not nudge me to sin, make me angry, or break my ear drums! Music, like the music David played for his sheep, that was a reprieve for a weary soul. A comfort and soothing balm running around in our minds, helping us to draw near to Him.

I just wanted to give these artists, and so many more a shout out. You will never know how much your music influenced my life, and so many others. Thank you for your sacrifices.

Question: Was there a person, group that meant a lot to you growing up?

lots o' dots!

"For I know the plans I have for you," declares the LORD, "plans to prosper you and not to harm you, plans to give you hope and a future."

Jeremiah 29:11 (NIV)

I was in the store looking over all the word and number games you can purchase to keep your mind sharp. There were crosswords, sudoku, mazes, word finds, hidden pictures, and so much more.

The one I was thinking about was the dot-to-dot, fun little puzzle drawing lines to connect dots. Most times, a picture will begin to appear as you begin to draw lines from one number to the next. Maybe a giraffe or tomato will start to become recognizable. When you do it correctly, it's fun to see the outcome. The outcome for the outline you draw has been predetermined by the designer of the game. If you started drawing your own dots in another pattern, well I'm not sure what you would come up with.

It's kind of the same with our lives. In the springtime, we have a lot of graduations. The ones most celebrated are preschool, middle-school, high school, and college. Up to the point of high school graduation, there are very few choices to make in our education. Oh, maybe you will choose an academic track of classes rather than a more "hands-on" track or technical track, but you will still be attending class, doing schoolwork, getting grades, etc. Once you graduate from high school, it may seem like you are outside the dots. You may feel that you are in an unfamiliar area with no dots to follow, and you are not sure if you will have a real picture for a grand finish. You are out there with no track to follow, no dots to draw the lines too! It can be a scary place! Yet, God says He knows the best plan for you. Seeking

God for that plan is the best way to be successful in life. I know this from experience. It took me a very long time before I paid attention and believed God had a better plan for me. Once we surrender our will to His, we can relax. The dots will appear again.

Following the dots God has for you is exciting and profitable. But those lots o' dots remind me of something a little more sinister that I want you to think about. Often in the news media we get conflicting reports on the very same question. It's confusing and frustrating. Not to mention the fact that it could really mess up some decision making on very important things when there is no straight forward consistent answer.

I'm afraid that after following the dots for at least twelve years in our school career, we are conditioned to continue on that path, no matter where it leads. Sometimes we need to shake ourselves to see where these new "dots" are really leading. Are we thinking before we follow or, have we forgotten how to think for ourselves and just follow the "dots?"

We have so much discord in our country right now about so many trains of thought. We need to know what the Bible says about any given topic. We need to follow those "dots," even if there is conflict. It will be far better for us at the gates of heaven when we can say, "I stood for what was right. I got here a little early, but it's okay. The alternative was to follow their dots, and I am pretty sure they were not leading to everlasting life."

Question: Take a few minutes and think about what topics are coming up right now in the news. What does the Bible say about each topic? Does the media align with the Biblical train of thought? Jeremiah 29:11 (NIV) says it best! Trust God for your future.

promises

And call on Me in the day of trouble; I will deliver you, and you will honor Me.

Psalm 50:15 (NIV)

I stood at the window, my tears flowing as quickly as the rain that pelted against the pane. How did I allow this to happen again? The date was set, the calendar marked, I am ready, and no show!

This was not the first time this happened to me. For years I had this same scenario play out over and over, yet every time I had hope that this time the promise would be kept.

How many of you can relate? A deadbeat dad that stood you up. A boyfriend that never even called. A promised check, bonus, trip, that never came. It all boils down to the same things: disappointment, a broken heart, a broken promise!

So, while it may take some time to trust again, you can trust the One who placed the stars and wrote the promises! He says, "Call on Me, I will deliver you in the day of trouble" (Psalm 50:15, NIV). Does He say you won't have trouble? No. In fact, He says in this world you *will* have trouble (John 16:33, NIV).

It's nice to receive a promise of something. Just don't depend on it too much! The promise giver is only human, after all. Trust in the Divine Promise Keeper. He will never stand you up; He will always deliver and never break your heart.

Question: What kind of a promise maker do you trust?

For further study, look up some promises God has made in the Bible.

afterword

If after you read these devotionals, you realize that you never really did give the reigns of your life to Jesus and you would like to, here is the process:

Acknowledge that Jesus is the only way you can be forgiven from your sin.

Confess to Him that you need His forgiveness and ask for it.

Believe that He has saved you from your sin, He has forgiven you, and He has promised to take you to Heaven when you die.

It is that simple! Now you are His child, and He is your personal Savior!

Sign and date this Confession of Faith to make it real in your life.

NAME

DATE
_____

Find and attend a local Bible believing church to build up your faith.

about the author

Donna studied Communications and Early Childhood Education at Marywood University. For over twenty-five years, she has held some type of Bible study for women and has organized several grass-roots conferences focusing on her love of the United States.

Over the years she has held many positions from Social Services Coordinator to second-grade teacher to window treatment fabricator. None have been as fulfilling as Mom, Nana and pastor's wife. Since she was in grade school, writing has always been a hobby, then a side job as a photojournalist for a local weekly neighborhood paper. Retiring has been the perfect time to write the book she always wanted to. You can contact her at: mydailyfirefly@gmail.com

1. Preston Ronald Liples eating PopPop's pancakes

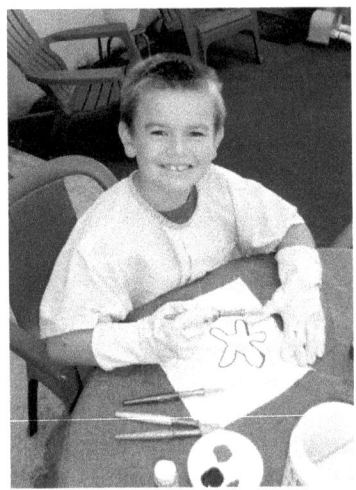

2. Grant William Liples working on his Masterpiece

3. Preston, Grant, Jaron, and Evan with Baba in the center. Baba is the author's mother and the children's great-grandmother

about the author

4. Cousins Preston and Evan Liples

5. Reverend Ron and Donna Liples

6. Author Donna M. Liples

7. Jaron Taylor Liples making the lilac's jealous

about the author

8. Evan James Liples ready to roll

Lightning Source UK Ltd.
Milton Keynes UK
UKHW011610160421
382096UK00009B/406